University of Wisconsin

Madison, WI

Written by Nicole Rosario

Edited by Alyson Pope and Jon Skindzier

Layout by Matt Hamman

Additional contributions by Omid Gohari, Christina Koshzow, Chris Mason, Joey Rahimi, and Luke Skurman

ISBN # 1-4274-0205-1
ISSN# 1552-1508
© Copyright 2006 College Prowler®
All Rights Reserved
Printed in the U.S.A.
www.collegeprowler.com

Last Updated 5/16/06

Special Thanks To: Babs Carryer, Andy Hannah, LaunchCyte, Tim O'Brien, Bob Sehlinger, Thomas Emerson, Andrew Skurman, Barbara Skurman, Bert Mann, Dave Lehman, Daniel Fayock, Chris Babyak, The Donald H. Jones Center for Entrepreneurship, Terry Slease, Jerry McGinnis, Bill Ecenberger, Idie McGinty, Kyle Russell, Jacque Zaremba, Larry Winderbaum, Roland Allen, Jon Reider, Team Evankovich, Lauren Varacalli, Abu Noaman, Mark Exler, Daniel Steinmeyer, Jared Cohon, Gabriela Oates, David Koegler, and Glen Meakem.

Bounce-Back Team: Bobak Roshan, Robert Chao, and Eric Miller.

College Prowler®
5001 Baum Blvd.
Suite 750
Pittsburgh, PA 15213

Phone: 1-800-290-2682
Fax: 1-800-772-4972
E-Mail: info@collegeprowler.com
Web Site: www.collegeprowler.com

Welcome to College Prowler®

During the writing of College Prowler's guidebooks, we felt it was critical that our content was unbiased and unaffiliated with any college or university. We think it's important that our readers get honest information and a realistic impression of the student opinions on any campus—that's why if any aspect of a particular school is terrible, we (unlike a campus brochure) intend to publish it. While we do keep an eye out for the occasional extremist—the cheerleader or the cynic—we take pride in letting the students tell it like it is. We strive to create a book that's as representative as possible of each particular campus. Our books cover both the good and the bad, and whether the survey responses point to recurring trends or a variation in opinion, these sentiments are directly and proportionally expressed through our guides.

College Prowler guidebooks are in the hands of students throughout the entire process of their creation. Because you can't make student-written guides without the students, we have students at each campus who help write, randomly survey their peers, edit, layout, and perform accuracy checks on every book that we publish. From the very beginning, student writers gather the most up-to-date stats, facts, and inside information on their colleges. They fill each section with student quotes and summarize the findings in editorial reviews. In addition, each school receives a collection of letter grades (A through F) that reflect student opinion and help to represent contentment, prominence, or satisfaction for each of our 20 specific categories. Just as in grade school, the higher the mark the more content, more prominent, or more satisfied the students are with the particular category.

Once a book is written, additional students serve as editors and check for accuracy even more extensively. Our bounce-back team—a group of randomly selected students who have no involvement with the project—are asked to read over the material in order to help ensure that the book accurately expresses every aspect of the university and its students. This same process is applied to the 200-plus schools College Prowler currently covers. Each book is the result of endless student contributions, hundreds of pages of research and writing, and countless hours of hard work. All of this has led to the creation of a student information network that stretches across the nation to every school that we cover. It's no easy accomplishment, but it's the reason that our guides are such a great resource.

When reading our books and looking at our grades, keep in mind that every college is different and that the students who make up each school are not uniform—as a result, it is important to assess schools on a case-by-case basis. Because it's impossible to summarize an entire school with a single number or description, each book provides a dialogue, not a decision, that's made up of 20 different topics and hundreds of student quotes. In the end, we hope that this guide will serve as a valuable tool in your college selection process. Enjoy!

OMID GOHARI ○ CHRISTINA KOSHZOW ○ CHRIS MASON ○ JOEY RAHIMI ○ LUKE SKURMAN ○
The College Prowler Team

Table of Contents

Introduction from the Author

Mention the University of Wisconsin to your peers, and watch their eyes light up with excitement. Responses will range from praise of the scenic locale to comments on its reputable social scene. Mention the school to your parents or teachers, and wait as they spout off facts about the amazing academics and educational aspects of UW. In either case, your audience will have something positive to say about your interest in the University.

While reputation is not the most important element of a school, it definitely tells you something about that university. Those attending UW hold high expectations of the education they'll receive, and the administration pushes intensely to meet those standards. Every department, from art history to organic chemistry, provides comprehensive knowledge through accessible instruction. Perhaps this is why UW continues to rank top in the nation for academic programs, as well as thrive in researching projects.

While you may feel that UW's academic reputation is all you need to know about, don't sell yourself short. UW is a school that encourages students to participate in more than just its classes. Student organizations, athletic teams, academic support groups, and campus social events are offered to further enrich and fulfill the undergraduate experience. Apart from excelling intellectually, the administration wants its students to nurture personal interests through extra-curricular activities.

All these facts are simply a start towards a full consideration of UW as your undergraduate choice. These next pages will give you an in-depth coverage on some of the collegiate aspects you may have overlooked. While reading through this book, I hope you gain a clearer picture of everything the University of Wisconsin stands to offer.

Nicole Rosario, Author
University of Wisconsin

By the Numbers

General Information

University of Wisconsin
500 Lincoln Dr.
Madison, WI 53706-1481

Control:
Public

Academic Calendar:
Semester

Religious Affiliation:
None

Founded:
1848

Web Site:
www.wisc.edu

Main Phone:
(608) 263-2400

Admissions Phone:
(608) 262-3961

Student Body

**Full-Time
Undergraduates:**
27,014

**Part-Time
Undergraduates:**
2,752

**Total Male
Undergraduates:**
13,932

**Total Female
Undergraduates:**
15,834

Admissions

Overall Acceptance Rate:
66%

Total Applicants:
20,495

Total Acceptances:
13,588

Freshman Enrollment:
5,642

Yield (% of admitted students who actually enroll):
41.5%

Early Decision Available?
No

Early Action Available?
No

Regular Decision Deadline:
February 1

Regular Decision Notification:
Varies by application

Must-Reply-By Date:
May 1

Waiting List Available?
No

Transfer Applications Received:
3,735

Transfer Applications Accepted:
1,819

Transfer Applicants Enrolled:
1,082

Transfer Applicant Acceptance Rate:
48%

Common Application Accepted?
Yes

Supplemental Forms?
Yes

Admissions E-Mail:
onwisconsin@admissions.wisc.edu

Admissions Web Site:
www.admissions.wisc.edu

SAT I or ACT Required?
Either

SAT I Range (25th–75th Percentile):
1160–1370

SAT I Verbal Range (25th–75th Percentile):
560–670

SAT I Math Range (25th–75th Percentile):
600–700

Retention Rate:
92%

Top 10% of High School Class:
58%

Application Fee:
$35

Financial Information

In-State Tuition:
$6,220

Out-of-State Tuition:
$21,060

Room and Board:
$6,500

Books and Supplies:
$860

**Average Need-Based
Financial Aid Package
(including loans, work-study,
grants, and other sources):**
$10,740

**Students Who Applied for
Financial Aid:**
53%

**Students Who
Received Aid:**
33%

Financial Aid Phone:
(608) 262-3060

Financial Aid E-Mail:
finaid@das.wisc.edu

Financial Aid Web Site:
www.finaid.wisc.edu

Academics

The Lowdown On...
Academics

Degrees Awarded:
Bachelor
Master
Post-Master Certificate
First Professional
First Professional Certificate
Doctorate

Most Popular Majors:
4% English
6% Political Science and
    Government
5% Psychology
4% Communication Studies
4% History

Undergraduate Schools:
College of Agricultural
and Life Sciences
College of Engineering
College of Letters and Science
Gaylord Nelson Institute for
Environmental Studies
School of Business
School of Education
School of Human Ecology
School of Journalism and
Mass Communication
School of Library and
Information Studies

(Undergraduate Schools, continued)

School of Medicine and Public Health
School of Music
School of Natural Resources
School of Nursing
School of Pharmacy
School of Social Work
School of Veterinary Medicine

Full-Time Faculty:
2,371

Faculty with Terminal Degree:
92%

Student-to-Faculty Ratio:
13:1

Average Course Load:
14 credits

Graduation Rates:
Four-Year: 43%
Five-Year: 75%
Six-Year: 79%

Special Degree Options

Individual major: this path allows students to have more control over their courses by choosing their core classes, versus taking ones required by the specific schools.

Departments like integrated liberal studies and women's studies offer certificates in their respective programs. These degrees are equivalent to minors at other schools.

AP Test Score Requirements

Possible credit for scores of 3–5, except for BC calculus test, which requires a 2 or better.

IB Test Score Requirements

Possible credit for scores of 4 or 5.

Did You Know?

Over **112 million dollars of financial aid** was awarded last year to undergraduate students attending the University of Wisconsin-Madison.

Second only to John Hopkins University, UW receives **the most federal aid grants** for research purposes.

First- and second-year students are eligible to partake in the Undergraduate Research Scholar program. URS allows students to **work hand in hand with UW faculty** on the latest studies in science, engineering, and humanities.

The National Academy of Science recently conducted a study of research-doctorate programs. Their results ranked **16 of UW's programs in the top 10**, and 35 in the top 25.

Sample Academic Clubs

Actuarial Science Club, Botany Club, Classics Club, European Union Club, Geriatrics Interest Group

Best Places to Study

Memorial Library Cages, College Library, Art Library, Helen C. White Library, and Steenbock Library

Students Speak Out On...
Academics

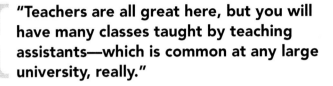

"Teachers are all great here, but you will have many classes taught by teaching assistants—which is common at any large university, really."

Q "Instructors are great depending on your year. Typical freshman and sophomore level lectures tend to be very large, so learning really takes place in the discussion classes led by TAs. **Sometimes, I feel a bit overwhelmed at the size of the classes**, but once you break down into discussions, it is normal. As you progress, your level of interaction with your professors increases, and you get more one-on-one time with them, which can either be good or bad."

Q "The professors are all right, but **it is a really hard school to begin with**, so don't expect them or the TAs to help you much. Madison gives you a lot of work, so expect to study at least a few hours a day."

Q "**It's really possible for you to get lost in a class and not have much contact with the professor**. You can get away with not doing the reading and all that good stuff if you want to go that route. But if you do want a more personal education or need any help, the professors are really good about that, and are more than happy to talk with you."

Q "The professors are excellent at UW. Unfortunately, when you are an undergraduate, you do not have much contact with your professors. It is all with the TAs. The professors teach the grad students who are the TAs. **I have worked with some professors though, and they are excellent**."

Q "The University of Wisconsin at Madison is ranked as one of the top thirty-five schools in America. It is regularly referred to as being among the finest of the state schools. **They have every major imaginable**, a course catalog that is phenomenal, and professors who can bring it all to life."

Q "I've had some very good teachers, and not one really bad teacher yet. I haven't gotten close to any of my professors, and I hope that happens next year. **Overall, I am satisfied here**."

Q "Being in the College of Engineering, I've gotten along well with my teachers so far. I was worried that instead of professors, I would get a lot of TAs to teach my classes, but this was not the case. **There is always someone around to help**—professors, TAs, tutors (which are free if you go through the university), and other options like voluntary lectures**.**"

Q "Most of my professors have been great, and so have the TAs. However, there are exceptions; some professors do not like to listen to their students as much as others do. Most all of my non-required classes have been very interesting. **One class project was brewing beer**!"

Q "**There are so many teachers that you will find both great and horrible ones**. Being at a very liberal campus, expect their viewpoints to be expressed, but not overbearingly so. The professors really do a good job at staying neutral."

Q "**For the first year or two, most of the classes are very large**, and students will not meet their professor unless a specific effort is made on the student's part. Most classes are interesting, yet I try and choose classes that will interest me. I don't find that the professors or the TAs are of a specific breed. They all seem to be different, and it is difficult to categorize and characterize them as something unique to Madison."

Q "It's hard to describe the teachers of this school since there are so many of them. Over the course of an education here, you're bound to find ones that you love, some that you hate, and many that you won't think either way about. **On the whole, though, they are excellent professors who make the material interesting** for their students, no matter the subject."

The College Prowler Take On...
Academics

Colleges attract students by promising high-quality academics and professional programs, and this is no different for the University of Wisconsin- Madison. With a school like the UW, however, its reputation for academic excellence almost precedes itself. Academically, many agree that one's first few years at UW will take place in large lecture rooms, with little acknowledgement from professors. In these beginning years, it is truly up to the students to stand out in the crowd and seek out professors if they are struggling. As the years pass and students get deeper into their major courses, their relationships with professors will become vital; however, if students find themselves not being able to get the professor's attention, try the class TAs. These instructors are usually graduate students, and understand students' needs first-hand.

The University of Wisconsin-Madison is ranked among the top 50 academic institutes in the nation, and many of its departments lead the country in education. Notably, the Business School is ranked third for their risk management program, and Engineering holds the same rank for their nuclear program. More so, UW offers academic programs in a variety of fields. Their liberal arts school is one of the largest in the Midwest, offering everything from creative writing to zoology. At UW, students can work towards their degree with confidence that they are receiving an excellent education.

B+

The College Prowler® Grade on

Academics: B+

A high Academics grade generally indicates that professors are knowledgeable, accessible, and genuinely interested in their students' welfare. Other determining factors include class size, how well professors communicate, and whether or not classes are engaging.

Local Atmosphere

The Lowdown On...
Local Atmosphere

Region:
Midwest

City, State:
Madison, WI

Setting:
Medium-sized city

Distance from Milwaukee:
2 hours

Distance from Chicago:
3 hours

Points of Interest:
Capital Square
State Street

Closest Shopping Malls:
East Towne Mall
University Square Mall
West Towne Mall

➜

Closest Movie Theaters:

University Square Theaters
62 University Square Mall
(608) 251-FILM

Orpheum Theater
216 State St.
(608) 255-8755

Local Financial Institutions:

CUNA Credit Union
First Federal
U.S. Bank
UW Credit Union

Major Sports Teams:

Green Bay Packers (football)
Milwaukee Brewers (baseball)
Milwaukee Bucks (basketball)

City Web Sites

www.ci.madison.wi.us
www.visit.madison.com
www.madison.com

Did You Know?

6 Fun Facts about Wisconsin:

- With Wisconsin being the leading producer of milk within the U.S., it is no wonder its residents consume almost **21 million gallons of ice cream** every year.

- "Wisconsin" is most likely an adaptation of the **Chippewa word _miskasinsin_**, meaning "red stone place," though others suggest it means "gathering of the waters," or "great rock."

- Over 15 cities in Wisconsin are considered "world capitals" for various products. For example, Monroe is known as the **World's Swiss Cheese Capital**, and Green Bay is the World's Toilet Paper Capital.

- Door County, an area spanning the upper east side of Wisconsin, has **250 miles of shoreline**. This is more shore than any other county in the United States.

- About **17 Nobel Prizes and 24 Pulitzer Prizes** have been awarded to UW faculty or its alumni.

- There are more than **15,000 lakes** throughout the state of Wisconsin. Surprisingly, this number is higher than their neighbor Minnesota, aka "the Land of 10,000 Lakes."

Famous People from Wisconsin:

Chris Farley – This young performer was best known for his comedy stunts on _Saturday Night Live_ and the big screen. He was the lovable lead in _Tommy Boy_ and _Black Sheep_.

Liberace – A famous musician during the '60s and '70s who created easy-listening tunes that will forever be remembered.

James Thomson – Leading the world in stem cell technology, Professor Thomson and his research group were first in the world to successfully isolate and culture human embryonic stem cells.

Famous People from Wisconsin, continued)

Orson Welles – Director of several films and a famous radio personality, Orson Welles is best known for his film, *Citizen Kane*. After its release, the American Film Institute elected it as "the greatest American film ever made."

Local Slang:

Bubbler – water fountain ("I need a drink from the bubbler.")

Cheese-head – Wisconsin native ("Oh, you're from Madison? You cheese-head!")

Doozy – unfortunate situation ("She dumped you, now that's a doozy!")

Disc-Golf – a hippie sport that incorporates golf and frisbee ("Wanna play a few rounds of disc-golf?")

Froke – past tense of freak ("I failed my test and froke out right in class.")

Jack – to assault or attack someone ("I'll jack you!")

Salty – a way one feels after being defeated ("After we lost at disc-golf I was feeling pretty salty.")

Soda – carbonated beverage ("To drink? I'll just have a soda.")

Tight – a phrase to show approval ("You have a date tomorrow?! Tight!")

Tyme Machine – ATM ("I need to get cash, where's the closest tyme machine?")

Students Speak Out On...
Local Atmosphere

"The atmosphere in Madison is pretty much anything goes. People do what they want and don't worry what others think of them. Protests are big in Madison. Student organizations are popular as well."

Q "The community is awesome here because it is totally a college town. But since it's the capitol of Wisconsin, there are a lot of important things and people here too. The campus is right between two big lakes, which makes it very nice in the summer when you can go to the Union and get a beer. **We were the first university in the country to sell beer at the student union**."

Q "**The atmosphere is two-fold**. It's a typical Midwestern city with a huge college in the middle. Wisconsin Dells is a great weekend getaway in the summer, and Tyrol Basin and Cascade Mountain are good ski areas. You definitely have to go to Summerfest in Milwaukee during the last week in June."

Q "**Madison is a very cool city**. It is small enough that it isn't overwhelming, but there is still tons of stuff to do all the time. There is a good live music scene."

Q "Also in Madison is Madison Area Technical College and Edgewood College, which are smaller. **The atmosphere is young, like a typical college town in a movie**. It is fun, with lots of outside activities and things to see, like the museum, the yearly film festival, and all kinds of plays."

Q "The great thing about Madison is that **it is a campus school, but it has all the amenities of a city**. There are movie theaters, restaurants, places to get lost when you want to think alone, and places to go to be surrounded by your peers. It has a very college feel. It is the only school I looked at that was a combination of a city and a campus."

Q "As far as actual looks go, **Madison is gorgeous**! It sits right on two lakes and one of our student unions has an amazing view. The snow is also pretty in the winter and the cold weather draws people together."

Q **"Stay away from anyone holding a cup on State Street**. Cross the street as many times as necessary to avoid 'Have any spare change?' Come on, I'm a college student, "spare" is not part of my vocabulary."

Q "My favorite spot is **on a sailboat in the middle of Lake Mendota**; beautiful skyline view**."

Q "The atmosphere is very college-esque. There are so many different groups of students that there is a somewhat diverse feeling to the town (if not racially diverse). **There is a very distinct feeling that the University dominates Madison**, or at least, the west side of the capital, with State Street playing a large part. There are a number of places to visit in and around the University, but they will most likely become some part of your routine in Madison, whether it be the various bars (a large number with varying atmospheres for all tastes) to local shops and restaurants."

Q "There are a few other universities, but they have no real presence. I would recommend Tenney Park for ice skating in the winter. **The geology museum is awesome**, too. We have a dinosaur there."

The College Prowler Take On...
Local Atmosphere

With two large lakes bordering opposite ends of campus and the Capital building sitting at the top of State Street, visually, there aren't enough positive things UW students can say about the locale of this college. Apart from the gorgeous aesthetics, students find the areas near campus to be very accessible. State St. offers a multitude of restaurants, shops, bars, and cafés. Capital Square also offers dinning and shopping, but at a little higher price. Students acknowledge the nearby universities, but at the same time, admit to not interacting with them much. In general, students feel the placement of campus creates a very picturesque and "college-esque" atmosphere.

Madison itself is a comfortably-sized city located in the heart of the Midwest. Most students feel its locality creates a friendly and safe environment. The UW campus sits right next to the city's trendiest street, complete with shops, restaurants, and bars. However, the campus is also close to a strong business district. The meshing of these two worlds exposes students to college life, and that of the 'real world'. Overall, students at Madison will be provided with the comforts of a small town, as well as the opportunities of a large city.

B

The College Prowler® Grade on
Local
Atmosphere: B

A high Local Atmosphere grade indicates that the area surrounding campus is safe and scenic. Other factors include nearby attractions, proximity to other schools, and the town's attitude toward students.

Safety & Security

The Lowdown On...
Safety & Security

Number of UW Police:
56

Madison Police Phone:
(608) 255-2345

UW Police Phone:
(608) 262-2957

Safety Services:
SafeWalks
October 1–March 31
7 p.m.–1 a.m
April 1–September 30
8 p.m.–1 a.m.

SafeCabs
9 p.m.–3 a.m.
9 p.m.–6 a.m. during final
exam periods
(608) 262-5000

(Safety Services, continued)

SafeBuses

Sunday—Thursday
6:30 p.m.–1:30 a.m., Friday–
Saturday 6:30 p.m.–3:00 a.m.

Health Services:

Clinical services, University
Pharmacy, SHIP Insurance

1552 University Ave.

(608) 265-5600

Counseling Services:

115 North Orchard St.

(608) 265-5600

Health Center Office Hours:

Monday–Tuesday
8:30 a.m.–5 p.m.,

Thursday–Friday
9 a.m.–5 p.m.

Did You Know?

College freshmen living in dorms are **nearly four times as likely as other undergrads to contract bacterial meningitis**, a potentially fatal disease which causes inflammation of the linings of the brain and spinal cord. If you plan on staying in the residence halls as a first-year student, the FDA and University Health Services highly recommend that you first receive the meningococcal vaccine Menactra.

Visit this page on the UHS Web site for more info:
www.uhs.wisc.edu/display_story.jsp?id=673&cat_id=38

Students Speak Out On...
Safety & Security

"I have never felt threatened here at all. There are programs where you can have people escort you back to your dorm if you feel unsafe, but you probably won't even need them—this campus is pretty safe."

Q "**Security is very, very good**. There is a very low crime rate on and off campus. Just like every other city, Madison has a few areas to stay away from, including South Park Street. Public emergency phones are all over campus, as well as an escort service to and from libraries late at night. They also have shuttles that run from Lakeshore dorms to State Street until 2 a.m."

Q "Security on campus is good. **There are safety phones all over campus**, and there are safety services if you stay out late like SafeWalk, where two students will come and meet you and walk you safely to where you want to go. There are also SafeCab and SafeBuses too."

Q "There is a program called SafeWalk, which allows people to be picked up by two other students and walked or driven anywhere on campus. **This is a very safe school**."

Q "I would avoid the Lakeshore Paths at night—they're **not especially well lit**. But in general, it is a very safe campus."

Q "Honestly, although it seems to be a flawed security system, **the bigger problems tend to happen outside of campus-patrolled areas**."

Q "The campus police are really prevalent, and I've noticed emergency phones on street corners, too, which are for immediate trouble. Every once in a while, you read in the papers about a sexual assault, but I think if you are smart and **don't put yourself in a bad situation**, then you'll have no problem at all."

Q "I have never felt unsafe at anytime in Madison. But at the same time, I have always stayed in the downtown Madison area. I would also assume that being a male might have something to do with it. I have never felt unsafe walking alone late at night, but out of common sense, **I would not encourage traveling alone late at night**, especially for females."

Q "I walked into this college with people telling me Madison is the one of the safest cities in the US. I realized later that this doesn't mean its 100 percent safe. **If you have a bike, own a bike lock**. Lock your door before you go out. I think that because theft happens so rarely, people are left off-guard, and lulled into a false sense of security."

Q "**I personally have not had any issues with security**, and Madison itself really hasn't either. Campus and dorm security itself is very efficient as well."

The College Prowler Take On...
Safety & Security

Location plays a large role in how students perceive safety at UW. Certain areas are a little less safe than others are, and students try to steer away from these. In general, students feel safe walking around campus, State Street, and near the dorms. Madison police along with Campus Police further ensure the safety by patrolling the campus and its surrounding areas. Furthermore, the more extreme crimes and incidents seem to take place farther from campus, and don't usually involve students.

Madison in general is a pretty safe city. Statistically, most criminal offenses fall into the larceny and theft category. Furthermore, the city generally falls under the national numbers for crime rates. Even so, common sense must be used when it comes to safety and security issues. UW offers numerous safety programs to assist individuals in certain situations. For example, students can call a free cab service to safely bring them home, or request an escort to walk them to their cars at night. The campus also has lit pathways throughout campus and emergency phones near the academic buildings.

A-

The College Prowler® Grade on

Safety & Security: A-

A high grade in Safety & Security means that students generally feel safe, campus police are visible, blue-light phones and escort services are readily available, and safety precautions are not overly necessary.

www.collegeprowler.com

Computers

The Lowdown On...
Computers

High-Speed Network?
Yes

Wireless Network?
Yes

Number of Labs:
13

24-Hour Labs?
No

Computer Lab Directory:
www.doit.wisc.edu/ computerlabs

Operating Systems:
Windows XP
Mac OS X
Linux

Discounted Software

DoIT recently signed purchasing discount contracts with Microsoft and Sun software for UW-Madison students. For example, students are able to purchase perpetual licenses for the latest Microsoft Office suites for Windows and Mac systems. For more specific deals contact the DoIT store.

Free Software

WiscWorld e-mail client

Charge to Print?

Varies between 4–25 cents a page.

Did You Know?

MyUW is an **personalized Web site available** to all students. This allows students to check grades, class times, financial aid status, union activities, and much more. Log on at *www.my.wisc.edu*.

For those needing to get away for the weekend but still wanting to stay on top of schoolwork, UW labs offer the perfect solution. **Students are able to rent wireless laptops for up to three days** through the various lab locations.

UW offers **free training sessions** for students wanting to learn things like basic computer software programs and Web design. There are also small workshops available for those interested on Photoshop, PowerPoint, and other specific computer programs.

Students Speak Out On...
Computers

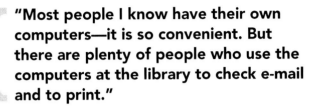

"Most people I know have their own computers—it is so convenient. But there are plenty of people who use the computers at the library to check e-mail and to print."

Q "If you have your own computer, you might as well bring it. When you live in the dorms, it is so easy to access the Internet and check your e-mail with the Ethernet connection. If you do not bring your computer, that's fine. There are plenty of computer labs and libraries all over campus. But **I highly recommend bringing your own**."

Q "Computer labs are busy, but you can pretty much always find a computer. The large majority of people have their own computers, so that is good too. I had one and it worked out well, but **it really doesn't make that much of a difference either way**."

Q "**There are tons of computer labs on campus**, and I've never not been able to get one if I needed to. The dorm network is great, and the off-campus cable and DSL are easily available."

Q "I would suggest bringing your own computer out of convenience. The labs are usually only crowded during exam times. The computer labs in the private dorms are never crowded, and you also get **free Internet in your room, so it was worth it** to have a computer."

Q "Bring a computer, but **buy a printer access card for last minute papers** when your printer runs out of ink at 2 a.m.!"

Q "We are a well-funded university, so we have tons of computer labs. **Don't worry about finding one**, especially if you live in the University dorms freshman year. All of them are equipped with computer labs either right in the building or below the cafeteria."

Q "**I brought my own computer to college and have yet to set foot in one of the University computer labs**. The [University] network is convenient, and anyone can access grades, register for classes, and look up school events online. If a student is living in the dorms, Internet access may be slower at certain points of the day, and the speed of file sharing programs is limited. But overall the network is fine."

Q "Just about every dorm has high speed Internet now. Though **I'd say its pretty much necessary to have a computer,** with the amount of web-based materials and research that many classes require. The computer labs aren't that bad, though, if you need them."

Q "Madison definitely isn't lacking in terms of computer labs. **We have over five libraries that are all well equipped with large computer labs**. They usually aren't crowded, except maybe around finals, but other than that you can usually find an open computer when you need it. Even so, if you can afford to have your own computer, I would suggest bringing one."

The College Prowler Take On...
Computers

While UW offers a plethora of computer labs and Internet access, the majority of students do bring their own computers, and suggest that others do as well. Students find convenience and safety in having a computer in their dorm room. This way, they can do their papers at their leisure, download music, and keep documents in a secure place. The dorms and private halls offer high-speed DSL in each room, along with small computer labs within the building. These smaller labs are nice if your computer is malfunctioning, or your printer runs out of ink and you're on a deadline. Be warned though—these smaller labs will often be crowded, and sometimes charge to print.

For those not able to bring their own computer, UW offers numerous labs spread all over campus. In order to meet the varying schedules of students, some open as early as six in the morning, while others stay open past midnight. All computer labs provide PC and Mac consoles so that students can use the programs they are most familiar and comfortable with. Furthermore, each lab is equipped with word-processing programs, Internet access, and research outlets. Along with these basic programs, the labs also provide printers, scanners, and copiers. For more specific computer hardware or software needs, check out the lab directory to find the right location.

The College Prowler® Grade on

Computers: B

A high grade in Computers designates that computer labs are available, the computer network is easily accessible, and the campus' computing technology is up-to-date.

Facilities

The Lowdown On...
Facilities

Student Centers:
Memorial Union
Union South

Athletic Centers:
Camp Randall Sports Center
Field House
Lathrop Hall
McClain Center
Natatorium
Porter Boathouse
Southeast Recreational
Facility (SERF)

Libraries:
35 on-campus libraries

Campus Size:
933 acres

Popular Places to Chill:
Bascom Hill
Library Mall
Student unions

What Is There to Do on Campus?

Visit the unions

Work out at the recreational centers

Go to the theaters

Movie Theater on Campus?

Memorial Union Theater

University Square Theaters

Bar on Campus?

Rathskeller in the Memorial Union

Union South

Coffeehouse on Campus?

College Library

Ingraham Hall

Memorial Union

Union South

Did You Know?

Camp Randall was once the site of a **Civil War training camp**. It now houses a 77,000 seat stadium and a memorial arch.

Students Speak Out On...
Facilities

{ **"The facilities on campus are great. All the buildings are in great condition, and our athletic buildings are some of the nicest in the country."**

Q "I enjoyed Memorial Union very much. There is nothing like sitting next to the lake on the Union Terrace, drinking a beer, and listening to a free concert. **There are lots of free shows**, and it's a good place to meet before going out, or just to sit and study when the weather is nice."

Q "**The facilities are very good**. There are a few workout facilities on campus and there are computers everywhere. There are two student centers, but we call them unions. There is the Memorial Union and Union South."

Q "The Memorial Union is a pretty cool place to go hang out, study, or eat. **It is right on the lake** and they usually have a lot of cool things going on there."

Q "Athletic facilities are the SERF, the Nat, and the Shell. SERF is for the southeast dorms and the Nat is for the lakeshore dorms. They have pretty much everything for athletics. The Shell, which is located in the southwestern part of campus near Camp Randall, is where the football team plays. **They are all fairly new and well-equipped**. There are computer labs everywhere, and most of the buildings on campus have at least a small lab. The problem is that you might have to wait for a computer, but they definitely have everything you need for schoolwork. The student unions aren't as big of a center for students as I've seen on other campuses."

Q "**The main union, Memorial Union, has the Rathskellar (a bar), a cafeteria, an arcade room, a pool, a terrace**, a student travel center, a movie theater, and many other things. There is another union near the engineering campus and it is smaller than Memorial Union. It has places to eat, club meeting rooms, pool, arcade games, and bowling. There is also a motel there."

Q "**I am satisfied with all campus facilities**, especially the Memorial Union and it's various clubs like the Hoofer Sailing Club."

Q "**The facilities are excellent**. We just finished adding an extension to our main athletic center, the SERF, and we have several others spread across campus. The computers are all fast, and the students centers are great places to do things, hang out by the lake, or play arcades."

Q "I find that the facilities on campus are more than acceptable, with conveniently located gyms, and the **main student union located very close to the center of campus**. It is hard to generalize all the buildings under one description because the buildings were built at various dates, and all have very different architectural styles."

Q "It's tough to ask for more when it comes to facilities. We have at least three fully-equipped and huge gyms for students to use, the SERF, the Shell and the Natatorium, and there are computer labs all over with good equipment. **The libraries are enormous** and a little daunting to find things in, but you won't want for more material.

Q "**This place is decked out**."

The College Prowler Take On...
Facilities

Students rave about the Memorial Union and it is by far one of the most attractive aspects of UW. It's comprised of the renowned Rathskellar bar, dining areas, a pool hall, and the lakeshore terrace. Students also enjoy heading to Union South for the bowling alley and lower-level dance club. While the athletic facilities do not receive as much praise, students do feel satisfied with what they offer. Both unions are on campus, and some athletic facilities are only a few blocks away.

While the unions and gyms are very popular, UW obviously has more to offer than just that—for example, the library system is extensive and spreads all over campus. There are a total of 35 libraries, and most are geared towards specific areas of study like geology or art history. Students find this very accommodating and accessible. The academic buildings are in good shape structurally and enhance student learning. For those studying law, the Foley & Lardner trial courtroom is in place for mock hearings and other legal proceedings. Those interested in the art field have access to the Elvejham museum; here, student art pieces are displayed and classes are taught. One negative aspect of some facilities, however, is the location. Since the school is several miles in size, some academic buildings or libraries may not be within walking distance, which can be inconvenient during bad weather.

The College Prowler® Grade on
Facilities: A-

A high Facilities grade indicates that the campus is aesthetically pleasing and well-maintained, facilities are state-of-the-art, and libraries are exceptional. Other determining factors include the quality of both athletic and student centers and an abundance of things to do on campus.

Campus Dining

The Lowdown On...
Campus Dining

Freshman Meal Plan Requirement?

No

24-Hour On-Campus Eating?

No

Meal Plan Average Cost:

No base fee, but UW recommends a minimum $500 deposit to your Housing Food account per semester

Places to Grab a Bite with Your Meal Plan:

Carson's Carryout

Food: Made-to-order, groceries

Location: 1515 Tripp Circle

Hours: Monday–Friday
11 a.m.–1:30 p.m.,
1:30 p.m.–5 p.m.
(groceries only),
5 p.m.–1 a.m.,
Saturday–Sunday
5 p.m.–1 a.m.

Chadbourne Cafeteria

Food: American

Location: Chadbourne Hall

Hours: Monday–Thursday
7 a.m.–10:30 a.m.,
11:15 a.m.–1:15 p.m.,
5 p.m.–6:45 p.m.,
Friday 7 a.m.–10:30 a.m.,
11:15 a.m.–1:15 p.m.,
5 p.m.–6 p.m.,
Saturday–Sunday
11:30 a.m.–12:30 p.m.,
5 p.m.–6 p.m.

Daily Dose

Food: Deli, grab-and-go

Location: Health Sciences Learning Center

Hours: Monday–Friday
7 a.m.–9 p.m., Saturday–Sunday 10 a.m.–6 p.m.

Daily Scoop

Food: Deli, grab & go

Location: Memorial Union

Hours: Monday–Friday
7:30 a.m.–9 p.m., Saturday–Sunday 12 p.m.–9 p.m.

Der Rathskellar

Food: Bavarian grill

Location: Memorial Union

Hours: Monday–Friday
7 a.m.–8 p.m.,
Saturday 8 a.m.–8 p.m.,
Sunday 11 a.m.–8 p.m.

Ed's Express

Food: Made-to-order, groceries

Location: 717 W Johnson St.

Hours: Monday–Friday
11 a.m.–1:30 p.m.,
1:30 p.m.–5 p.m.
(groceries only),
5 p.m.–1 a.m.,
Saturday–Sunday
11:30 a.m.–5 p.m.
(groceries only),
5 p.m.–1 a.m.

Feed Bag Deli

Food: Deli, grab-and-go

Location: School of Veterinary Medicine

Hours: Monday–Friday
7:45 a.m.–1:45 p.m.

Food Court at Einstein's

Food: Asian, Mexican, pizza, potato bar, bistro

Location: Union South

Hours: Monday–Friday
11 a.m.–2 p.m.

Frank's Place

Food: American

Location: Kronshage Hall

Hours: Monday–Friday
7 a.m.–8:30 p.m.,
Saturday–Sunday
10 a.m.–8:30 p.m.,
Sunday–Thursday
8:30 p.m.–11:30 p.m.
(late-night dining)

Grainger Deli

Food: Deli, grab-and-go

Location: First and third
floors of Grainger Hall

Hours: Monday–Friday
7:30 a.m.–11 a.m. (first floor),
Monday–Friday 11 a.m.–
2:30 p.m. (third floor)

ICU Deli

Food: Deli, grab-and-go

Location: Medical sciences
building

Hours: Monday–Friday
7 a.m.–3 p.m.

Ingraham Deli

Food: Deli, grab-and-go

Location: Ingraham Hall

Hours: Monday–Friday
7 a.m.–3 p.m.

Lakefront on Langdon

Food: Wraps, Chinese, grill

Location: Memorial Union

Hours: Monday–Friday
11 a.m.–7 p.m., Sunday
8 a.m.–1 p.m.

Liz Waters

Food: American

Location: Elizabeth
Waters Hall

Hours: Monday–Thursday
7 a.m.–10:30 a.m.,
11:15 a.m.–1:15 p.m.,
5 p.m.–6:45 p.m.,
Friday 7 a.m.–10:30 a.m.,
11:15 a.m.–1:15 p.m.,
5 p.m.–6 p.m.,
Saturday–Sunday
11:30 a.m.–12:30 p.m.,
5 p.m.–6 p.m.

Open Book Café

Food: Deli, grab-and-go

Location: Helen C.
White building

Hours: Monday–Wednesday
10 a.m.–2 a.m.,
Thursday 10 a.m.–12 a.m.,
Friday 10 a.m.–9 p.m.,
Saturday 12 p.m.–9 p.m.,
Sunday 12 p.m.–12 a.m.

Pop's Club

Food: American

Location: 717 W Johnson St.

Hours: Monday–Friday
7 a.m.–8:30 p.m., Saturday–
Sunday 10 a.m.–8:30 p.m.

Quick Byte Deli

Food: Deli, grab & go

Location: Union South

Hours: Monday–Friday
7 a.m.–9 p.m., Saturday–
Sunday 10 a.m.–8 p.m.

Red Oak Grill

Food: American, grill

Location: Union South

Hours: Monday–Friday
7 a.m.–8 p.m.,
Saturday 8 a.m.–4 p.m.

Student Favorites:

Chadbourne Cafeteria

Pop's Club

Off-Campus Places to Use Your Meal Plan:

You can use your meal plan at any of the restaurants on State Street.

See the off-campus dining section for listings.

Did You Know?

Ed's Express and Carson's Carryout allow you to **order meals and groceries online**. This way, you can avoid the lunchtime rush, delayed services, and ala carte lines. Online ordering is a great way to save and budget your time.

Students Speak Out On...
Campus Dining

{

"The food in the cafeteria is all right—it's cheap if you eat in the dorms. Other places like the Union, or anywhere on State Street, are really good."

Q "The restaurants I like to go to are Porta Bella on State Street, and Old Chicago on West Towne. There is also the Parthenon for gyros, and the Blue Moon Bar and Grill on University Avenue for bar food. Gumby's Pizza is good for late-night drunk food. **Madison has a great variety**."

Q "Both student unions (Memorial Union and Union South) **offer great meal plans** for those students living off campus."

Q "**The food on campus is great**! There are some excellent restaurants on State Street. My favorites are Tutto Pasta, Noodles & Co, and Qdoba. You will love State Street— there are so many cute stores and exotic restaurants!"

Q "There are lots of places to eat on campus. **Dorm food is so-so, but what can you expect**? The restaurants on State Street are very good. I eat there all the time. I recommend Qdoba, Noodles & Co., and Spice's Kitchen."

Q "Food on campus is great. The food in the dorms isn't bad, and **there are tons of awesome restaurants within 10 minutes of walking**. Most restaurants stay open late, so there is plenty of food available late at night."

Q "The food on campus isn't that great. I lived in the private dorms, and **I heard that it is better in the public dorms, because you have more choices**."

Q "The dining hall serves just that—dining hall food. **It's not great, occasionally horrible, but mediocre overall**. The interesting thing about the dining hall is that they have cards with nutrition facts in front of whatever food you pick. That is so you truly know how many grams of fat you are taking in with your over-processed food."

Q "It pretty much goes without saying that most people aren't going to like their dining hall's food. Despite that, from what I've seen, they have decent things to eat. **If you have a taste for anything at all, State Street has it**."

Q "State Street has Afghani, African, Mexican, Italian, Indian, Persian, Chinese and Japanese restaurants all over. **And there's a McDonald's if you don't like culture**. Honestly, the best way to experience food in this town is to just walk down the street and get a table at whatever restaurant you haven't eaten at yet. Odds are you'll love it, and you can go for literally a month eating out every day before you have to eat the same kind of food twice."

The College Prowler Take On...
Campus Dining

Try as they might, students cannot mask the inevitable, and universal, disappointment in campus dining. Public and private dorms do provide meal plans and try to meet the appetites of their residents. Most halls will offer a variety of main entrees along with vegetarian options. Students will admit that dorm cafeterias are convenient for location, price, and student socialization. However, students did have a little bit more to say about the alternatives to dorm food. It seems if given the option to ditch the dorm meals, they will gladly take it.

While the dorm food options may be minimal, UW does offer a fair amount of dinning locations. The private dorms all have on-site cafeterias, and meal plans that transfer to the other private dorms. Public dorms, however, vary in dining locations; some have on-site cafés and some don't. Hours of service vary as well. The majority of the dorms have specific times when breakfast, lunch, and dinner are served and those coming in late are out of luck. For those not able to make the regulated mealtimes try the on-campus alternatives like Pop's Club or Ed's Express. Their hours don't directly coincide with dorm cafés, and tend to be open later as well. Make sure to check your hall's meal plan, though, for specifications.

The College Prowler® Grade on
Campus Dining: C+

Our grade on Campus Dining addresses the quality of both school-owned dining halls and independent on-campus restaurants as well as the price, availability, and variety of food.

Off-Campus Dining

The Lowdown On...
Off-Campus Dining

Restaurant Prowler:
Popular Places to Eat!

Amy's Cafe
Food: American, Greek
414 W Gilman St.
(608) 255-8172
www.amyscafe.com
Cool Features: Amy's offers American-style cuisine with a Mediterranean flair.
Price: $10 per person
Hours: Daily 11 a.m.–10 p.m.

Buffalo Wild Wings (BW3)
Food: Wings, burgers
529 State St.
(608) 255-9464
www.buffalowildwings.com
Cool Features: This sports bar has two levels of seating, with large television monitors to show the day's biggest sporting event.
Price: $10 per person
Hours: Sunday–Thursday 11 a.m.–2:30 a.m., Friday–Saturday 11 a.m.–3 a.m.

The Casbah Restaurant

Food: Mediterranean cuisine

119 E Main St.

(608) 255-2272

*www.thecasbah
restaurant.com*

Cool Features: Located near the capital, this low-lit restaurant offers three separately themed dining levels. For a special occasion order a hookah and try King Tut's lower seating.

Price: $10 per person

Hours: Monday–Wednesday 11 a.m.–9 p.m., Thursday–Saturday 11 a.m.–2 a.m., Sunday 5 p.m.–9 p.m.

Chin's Asia Fresh

Food: Chinese

422 State St.

(608) 661-0177

www.chins.com

Cool Features: Chin's food isn't just cheap and fresh, it's healthy, too.

Price: $10 per person

Hours: Daily 11 a.m.–9 p.m.

Einstein Bros. Bagels

Food: Sandwiches, bagels

652 State St.

(608) 257-9828

www.einsteinbros.com

(Einstein Bros. Bagels, continued)

Cool Features: There aren't many surprises here, though every few months they will come out with a featured bagel that is worth a try.

Price: $6 per person

Hours: Monday–Saturday 7 a.m.–7 p.m., Sunday 7 a.m.–3 p.m.

Ian's Pizza & Salad

Food: Pizza

119 State St.

(608) 442-3535

www.ianspizza.com

Cool Features: How can you go wrong with pizza toppings like macaroni and cheese, guacamole burrito, and BBQ chicken and pineapple?

Price: $10 per person

Hours: Monday–Saturday 11 a.m.–2 a.m., Sunday 12 p.m.–10 p.m.

Noodles & Company

Food: Asian to Italian pastas

232 State St.

(608) 257-6393

Cool Features: This restaurant seems to be all-over the country. This particular location has two levels and a view of upper State Street.

(Noodles & Company, continued)

Price: $8 per person

Hours: Sunday–Wednesday 11a.m.–9 p.m., Thursday–Saturday 11 a.m.–10 p.m.

Qdoba

Food: Mexican

548 State St.

(608) 280-8720

http://qdoba.com

Cool Features: This is a late-night favorite. You can always find a spot to sit, and sometimes even someone you know. During the warm seasons, they offer outside seating and cold Coronas.

Price: $8 per person

Hours: Monday-Thursday 10:30 a.m.–3 a.m., Friday–Saturday 10:30 a.m.–3 a.m., Sunday 10:30 a.m.–1 a.m.

Potbelly Sandwich Works

Food: sandwiches, soups

564 State St.

(608) 259-9553

www.potbelly.com

Cool Features: This place is known for their inventive sandwiches, delicious shakes, and flavorful soups at a quality price.

(Potbelly Sandwich Works, continued)

Price: $7 per person

Hours: Daily 11 a.m.–11 p.m.

Sunroom Café

Food: Coffee, breakfast

638 State St.

(608) 255-1555

Cool Features: This restaurant is a must for morning-lovers. The windows are tall and capture exceptional morning light, hence its name.

Price: $8 per person

Hours: Daily 7 a.m.–9 p.m.

Tutto Pasta Trattoria

Food: Authentic Italian dishes

305 State St.

(608) 294-1000

Cool Features: Students enjoy the festive scenery and extensive wine list. This is a great place for a night out with friends, or if on a date.

Price: $10–$15 per person

Hours: Sunday–Thursday 11 a.m.–1 a.m., Friday–Saturday 11 a.m.–2 a.m.

Closest Grocery Store:
Capital Food Center

24-Hour Eating:
No

Late-Night Specials:
The Casbah Restaurant

Qdoba

Student Favorites:
Qdoba

Chin's Asia Fresh

Buffalo Wild Wings

Tutto Pasta

Best Pizza:
Ian's Pizza & Salad

Best Chinese:
Chin's Asia Fresh

Best Breakfast:
Sunroom Café

Best Wings:
Buffalo Wild Wings

Best Healthy:
Chin's Asia Fresh

Best Place to Take Your Parents:
Tutto Pasta Trattoria

Other Places to Check Out:
Blue Moon Bar & Grill

Brat House

Continental Café and Pastry Shop

Delmonico's

Great Dane Pub & Brewery

Gumby's Pizza

Madison's Dining & Diversions

Ocean Grill

Old Chicago

Outback Steakhouse

Paison's

Parthenon-Gyros

Porta Bella Italian Restaurant

Restaurant Magnus

Spice's Kitchen

Stillwaters, Inc.

Taco Johns

Takara Japanese Restaurant

Tornado Club Steak House

Did You Know?

Each year towards the end of August, the city hosts the Taste of Madison. This fair of food is held on the capital loop, and offers samples of historic Wisconsin dishes along with the cuisine of local restaurants. Be sure to try a bite!

Students Speak Out On...
Off-Campus Dining

"There are an unlimited number of places to go. Madison has something like the second-largest restaurant-per-capita in the United States."

Q "My favorite restaurant off-campus is Noodles, which serves pasta, and there are a bunch of other good ones, like Sunroom Café and Amy's Café."

Q "You've got your fast-food and then your normal restaurants. I like Madison's downtown area more because it is bigger, and there is more to choose from."

Q "If you have a car there are tons of good places out by East Town Mall, like the Outback Steakhouse."

Q "Restaurants in the downtown area consist of everything someone could have a craving for, and prices range accordingly; the closer to the capital, usually the steeper the price. Some good spots include Qdoba (cheap tex-mex burritos), Noodles (cheap assorted noodles), Potbelly's (cheap hot sandwiches), Amy's Café (cheap assorted sandwiches with a semi-Mediterranean menu), Madison's Dining and Diversions (reasonably priced assorted menu), the Great Dane (reasonably priced burgers), Ocean Grill (somewhat expensive seafood), and Takara (somewhat expensive sushi and hibachi)."

Q "If you are looking for high class, look around the capital area, which has a ton of great restaurants such as the Tornado Club."

Q "**Madison has the most restaurants-per-capita in the Midwest**. State Street is the place to go for food. BW3's is a great wing place, Qdoba is an awesome Mexican/taco place, and if you like noodles, there is Noodles & Company. Many great restaurants are all in a short proximity to each other."

Q "**The restaurants by the capital are all good**, notably the Magnus and the Casbah."

Q "Madison also has a lot of different ethnic spots. The Casbah has an unbelievable Mediterranean cuisine. **Some restaurants are more expensive than others**, but then it gives you the option of going somewhere swanky for a nice occasion."

The College Prowler Take On...
Off-Campus Dining

When dorm food fails to spark an interest, many students find themselves wandering up and down State Street looking for a more fulfilling alternative. However, students advise that if you are hunting for food during the lunch hours, be prepared for a wait. Places like McDonalds, Einstein Bros. Bagels, Noodles & Company, and Qdoba have the longest lines. If you do have a little more time, though, students suggest trying a sit-down restaurant like Stillwater's. Apart from the everyday eateries, Madison does offer an array of fancier, more occasion-based restaurants. Near the capital are some elegant spots that allow students to dress up and enjoy the time. Try out Delmonico's or Continental Café; both these places have great ambiance and expansive wine lists.

The areas surrounding campus are filled with every type of cuisine imaginable. Students can usually find food at an affordable price. The lower half of State Street offers chain restaurants and fast food joints. For nicer places, students travel farther up State Street and towards capital square. Another place offering a variety of food venders is University Square. Located one block from State Street, this mall plaza houses about five cozy restaurants. Those with a car, though, are truly in luck. The malls are only 15 minutes away with tons of eating options.

B

The College Prowler® Grade on

Off-Campus
Dining: B

A high Off-Campus Dining grade implies that off-campus restaurants are affordable, accessible, and worth visiting. Other factors include the variety of cuisine and the availability of alternative options (vegetarian, vegan, Kosher, etc.).

Campus Housing

The Lowdown On...
Campus Housing

Undergrads Living on Campus:
24%

Room Types:
Single
Double
Triple
Suite

Number of Dormitories:
17

Number of University-Owned Apartments:
2

University Apartments Office:
(608) 262-3407

Best Dorm:
Lakeshore Dorms

Worst Dorm:
Ogg Hall

Dormitories:

Adams Hall

Floors: Four 4-story buildings

Total Occupancy: 275

Bathrooms: Communal

Coed: By alternating floor

Residents: Mostly freshmen

Room Types: Single, double, suite

Special Features: Kitchen, den, laundry room, game room, study lounges, volleyball courts

Barnard Hall

Floors: 5

Total Occupancy: 138

Bathrooms: Communal

Coed: By wing on floors 2, 3, and 4; floors 1 and 5 are all female

Residents: Mostly freshmen

Room Types: Single, double, suite

Special Features: Chadbourne cafeteria, lounge, dens, music practice room, laundry room

Bradley Learning Community

Floors: 4

Total Occupancy: 246

Bathrooms: Communal

Coed: By wing

Residents: Mostly freshmen

Room Types: Doubles

(Bradley Learning Community, continued)

Special Features: Bradley Roundtable (a one-credit course that attempts to recreate the classic Greek symposium through dinner and discussion), reserved class selections, cross-college advising office

Chadbourne Residential College

Floors: 10

Total Occupancy: 688

Bathrooms: Communal

Coed: By alternating floor

Residents: Various

Room Types: Double, triple

Special Features: Chadbourne cafeteria, cross-college advising office, computer lab, reserved class selection, kitchen

Cole Hall

Floors: 4

Total Occupancy: 244

Bathrooms: Communal

Coed: No

Residents: All female

Room Types: Double

Special Features: TV/study lounge, kitchen, dens, laundry room, music practice room, game room, resources for Women in Science and Engineering (WISE)

Eagle Heights

Floors: Several 2–3 story buildings; 1044 apartments

Total Occupancy: 1848

Bathrooms: Private

Coed: Yes

Residents: Graduate and professional students, and student families

Room Types: 1-, 2-, and 3-bedroom apartments

Special Features: Storage lockers, laundry room; all apartments come with refrigerator, stove/oven, and garbage disposal

Elizabeth Waters Hall

Floors: 4

Total Occupancy: 488

Bathrooms: Communal

Coed: No

Residents: All female

Room Types: Double

Special Features: Kitchen, TV/study lounges, dens, laundry room, WISE resource room, reserved class selections, exercise room, parlor, music practice room, computer lab, terraces overlooking the lake

Fredrick House

Floors: 4, floors 1–3 are reserved for University visitors

Total Occupancy: 50

Bathrooms: Private

(Fredrick House, continued)

Coed: By alternating room

Residents: Upperclassmen

Room Types: Double

Special Features: Lakeshore location, conference rooms, option to participate in Alexander Meiklejohn Residential College

Harvey Street Apartments

Floors: Seven 2-story buildings; 47 apartments

Total Occupancy: Varies

Bathrooms: Private

Coed: Yes

Residents: Single graduate and professional students

Room Types: 1- and 2-bedroom apartments

Special Features: All apartments come with refrigerator, stove/oven, garbage disposal, and simple furnishings (couch, tables, chairs, lamps, dresser, desk); heat and electricity are included in rent

Kronshage Hall

Floors: Seven 3-story buildings

Total Occupancy: 616

Bathrooms: Communal

Coed: By alternating floor

Residents: Mostly freshmen

Room Types: Double

(Kronshage Hall, continued)

Special Features: Fireplace, study lounges, kitchen, computer lab, in-hall classrooms, laundry rooms, music practice hall

Merit House

Floors: 3

Total Occupancy: 63

Bathrooms: Private

Coed: By suite

Residents: Freshmen and upperclassmen

Room Types: Double, suite

Special Features: Laundry room, storage, rec lounge

Ogg Hall

Floors: Two 12-story buildings

Total Occupancy: 948

Bathrooms: Communal

Coed: By alternating floor

Residents: Mostly freshmen

Room Types: Double

Special Features: Game room, fireplace, study lounge, dens, laundry room, music practice room, storage space, in-hall classroom, kitchen, front desk offers movies, sports equipment, and board games for rent, cross-college advising office, reserved class selection, first-year interest group (FIG)

Sellery Hall

Floors: Two 9-story buildings

Total Occupancy: 1148

Bathrooms: Communal

Coed: By wing

Residents: Mostly freshmen

Room Types: Double

Special Features: TV/study lounges, dens, clubhouse, movie/game rentals, kitchen, laundry, backyard, music practice room, residence life office, cross-college advising office, in-hall classroom, reserved course selection

Slichter Hall

Floors: 4

Total Occupancy: 200

Bathrooms: Communal

Coed: By wing

Residents: Freshmen and upperclassmen

Room Types: Double

Special Features: Kitchen, music dens, laundry rooms, game room, movie, game, and sports equipment rentals

Smith Hall

Floors: 6

Total Occupancy: 414

Bathrooms: Shared by groups of five residents

Coed: By every five resients

Residents: Mostly upperclassmen

(Smith Hall, continued)

Room Types: Single, double

Special Features: Soundproof music room, technology center, in-hall classrooms, cross-college advising office

Sullivan Hall

Floors: 4

Total Occupancy: 259

Bathrooms: Communal

Coed: By wing

Residents: Various

Room Types: Double

Special Features: Dens, study lounge, music practice room, game room, front desk provides movie, game, and sports equipment rentals

Susan B. Davis House

Floors: 3

Total Occupancy: 30

Bathrooms: Communal

Coed: By alternating floor

Residents: Mostly upperclassmen

Room Types: Single

Special Features: Study/rec lounge, kitchen, laundry room

Tripp Hall

Floors: 4

Total Occupancy: 280

Bathrooms: Communal

Coed: By alternating floor

Residents: Mostly upperclassmen

Room Types: Single, double

Special Features: Dens, study lounge, laundry room, billiards, music practice room

Witte Hall

Floors: Two 9-story buildings

Total Occupancy: 1150

Bathrooms: Communal

Coed: By wing

Residents: Mostly freshmen

Room Types: Double

Special Features: Substance-free option, dens, study lounge, in-hall classroom, kitchen, music practice room, dark room, laundry rooms, storage space, ATM, backyard, cross-college advising office

What You Get

Bed, desk, dressers and shelving, Internet-ready rooms, phone line with voice messaging, basic cable, computer labs with DSL, entertainment rooms, study rooms

Bed Type

Twin or full

Available for Rent

Movies, video games, board games, and sports equipment can be rented at the front desk of many residence halls

Cleaning Service?

A cleaning company maintains the common areas

Also Available

Those needing two parking spaces may obtain a second one for a fee

Web Site

www.housing.wisc.edu/assignment/communities

Did You Know?

Many public and private dorms contract with outside **laundry services**. Students are then able to have their laundry collected, washed, dried, and then delivered back to them within three days.

If you know a friend who plans on attending UW, you two can room together simply by requesting each other as roommates. For those who leave it up to the school to choose a roomie— have no fear! Every student completes a survey to asses his/ her personality and pairs them with the **best possible match**.

> **"If you are a freshman, I would recommend living in the Southeast dorms—Sellery, Ogg, Witte. They are right near everything. I lived in Ogg my freshman year, and I had the best time of my life."**

Q "**I would put my plug in for the Lakeshore dorms**. I have lived in Kronshage and Slichter Halls. I loved being by the lakes and being able to go rollerblading, biking, and swimming all within a block of where I lived. The Lakeshore dorms are set in the trees on the shore of Lake Mendota. It's quiet and secluded, yet very close to everything."

Q "I live in Chadbourne and I really like it. **There are lots of cool people, and I like the atmosphere**. There is a lot to get involved in."

Q "**Dorms are dorms**. You won't be happy to be in them, but everyone has to go through it. I recommend living in either Sellery or Witte, because they are much more social. If you want quiet, choose one of the Lakeshore dorms."

Q "I lived in the Witte dorm. I got the impression that most dorm rooms are the same no matter where you go. I think that Lakeshore dorm rooms are a little smaller and older. The Southeast dorms—Witte, Sellery, and Ogg—are newly renovated. Anyway, I liked them; they're within a ten-minute walk to most of the campus. Lakeshore is about the same. **Take your pick. They're both just fine**."

Q "The dorms are small but nice. The Lakeshore dorms are very nice, and kind of cottage-like. However, they are a little further away but right on the lake! For freshmen, I would suggest Witte and Sellery. **They are the fun ones where freshmen live**, and you'll meet a lot of people there. The Lakeshore dorms are a little more chill and quiet."

Q "**Every dorm will be fun, because you will make friends**. However, I wouldn't live in an all-girls dorm. Dorm living is part of the experience of being a freshman in college."

Q "**If you want party dorms,** then live in Southeast (Ogg, Witte, Sellery). If you want nicer dorms, then you want to live in Lakeshore (TAS, Kronshage). Southeast is closer to State Street, while Lakeshore is really far from it."

Q "The private dorms (I lived in the towers) are **mostly kids from the East Coast, Chicago, California**, and any other big city."

Q "I live in Kronshage, which is on the Lakeshore side of campus. The rooms are a little bigger, and you can arrange your room more than you can in the Southeast dorms. **It is quieter out there, so you can study on the weeknights if you need to**. Plus, buses stop right there, so it's not a big deal to get around campus."

Q "For the Southeast dorms, don't stay in Ogg. The rooms are a little smaller, and it is a lot louder. On the weekends, a lot more drunken vandalism goes on there. However, it is closer to State Street and the weekend social scene. For Lakeshore, I'd suggest staying in Slichter or Kronshage. For Southeast, pick Sellery, then Witte. **Ogg is the worst dorm on campus, in my opinion**."

Q "**The dorms are all nice**. Avoid the Towers unless you are planning on joining a frat, or unless you are from the East Coast. The Langdon is nice, clean, and has decent food."

Q "The dorms are small, crowded, loud. Although one would never choose to live in them again, **as most students move out after freshman year**, it is an experience few would be willing to pass up."

Q "Dorms are always filled with a mix of people you will and won't get along with. **The public dorms are the most unpredictable assortment of people**, so the people in them can't really be generalized. I've noticed that the PRH dorms are generally more laid back. The Lakeshore dorms are a long way away, and if you want a quiet atmosphere to live in, that would be your choice."

The College Prowler Take On...
Campus Housing

UW students have a complete range of options when it comes to on-campus living. When choosing a dorm, location sometimes becomes the largest factor. Students suggest that those looking to stay closer to academic buildings should try Chadbourne or Liz Waters. Both are right on campus and offer extraordinary academic support programs. If students are looking for a little more lax or social atmosphere, the Southeast dorms are the place to be. In terms of pure appearance, students can't go wrong with the Lakeshore dorms. These cottage-like buildings border Lake Mendota, offering a phenomenal view and country atmosphere.

UW is very accommodating in terms of student housing. There are thirteen public (University) dorms, and about five private dorms. The public dorms are primarily for freshmen and sophomores looking to meet people, and wanting to ease into college life. They all have computer labs, laundry facilities, study rooms, and entertainment lounges. Each also has something unique about it, either in terms of academics or campus involvement. Amenities and pricing do vary, so be sure to fully check out all options before finalizing any living situation. While some of your better days may not be spent in the dorms, the majority defend this housing option.

The College Prowler® Grade on

Campus Housing: B-

A high Campus Housing grade indicates that dorms are clean, well-maintained, and spacious. Other determining factors include variety of dorms, proximity to classes, and social atmosphere.

Off-Campus Housing

The Lowdown On...
Off-Campus Housing

Undergrads in Off-Campus Housing:
76%

Average Rent For:
Studio Apt.: $400
1 BR Apt.: $500
2 BR Apt.: $700

For Assistance Contact:
Steve Brown Apartments
(608) 255-7100
www.stevebrownapts.com

Popular Areas:
Langdon St.
Henry St.
Gilman St.
Gorham St.
University Ave.
Mifflin St.

Best Time to Look for a Place:
November–March

Students Speak Out On...
Off-Campus Housing

"Off-campus housing is extremely convenient, since everyone except freshmen live off campus. It is easy to find a house within walking distance of classes. Expect to have to walk 15–20 minutes to classes from anywhere."

Q "Madison is a big campus, and the farther you live, the **farther you are going to have to walk to class.**"

Q "Off-campus housing is very abundant. **I would stay away from the big off-campus dorms**, since they tend to be a rip-off. Also, I would say live in the dorms for at least a year. I lived in the dorms for two years and met a lot of my very close friends there. Orchard Street is a very popular area, as well as Langdon Street, which is a Greek area and close to State Street."

Q "**Housing off campus is everywhere**. You can find a nice place, which is expensive, or you can live with seven kids in a dump, which is what I'm doing next year, and that's cheap—$250 a month. But you'll pay utility charges, too, when you're out of the dorms, and you'll have to buy groceries."

Q "There's plenty of places to rent, and a huge choice if you look early enough. You want to live in the dorms freshman year, but if you want to live off campus sophomore year, **you should start looking for places during your freshman fall semester.**"

Q "This coming school year, I'm planning on housing off-campus at an apartment right near Langdon St.reet. It is close to the fraternities and close to State Street bars. Since I dormed near there my first year, classes won't be much different in terms of walking distance. I have checked out a few other apartments, but didn't enjoy them as much, since **location is very important** to me."

Q "There are tons of apartments off campus. After freshman year, **most students live off campus**."

Q "**I couldn't be anywhere else**. I live on State Street, all utilities paid, three blocks from the Union, across the street from Brats, down the street from Blockbuster, Mondays, and BW3's."

Q "Off-campus housing is worth it, and with the right number of roommates in the right location, **it can be cheaper than dorms**. There is plenty of non-university housing, and it is merely a matter of when one starts looking, whether or not roommates are planned out, and how much one is willing to pay. The privacy, independence, and increased square footage all play into the advantages of not living in the dorms."

Q "You almost **have to live off campus** after your freshman year. It is very convenient and readily available."

Q "If you're going to get an apartment, make sure you're doing it with a group of friends. Housing on campus is ridiculously expensive, and **the more friends you have, the less your wallet cries**. One bit of advice before moving in with people—make absolutely sure you know them. I've seen so many friendships shatter just because people moved in together."

The College Prowler Take On...
Off-Campus Housing

While it is definitely beneficial to spend at least a year in the dorms, off-campus housing is highly recommended. Madison has a plethora of houses, apartment buildings, and co-ops for students to live in. The general rule is that the closer you are to campus, the more you're going to pay. These areas include Langdon Street, Gorham Street, Gilman Street, and University Avenue. For some, though, being two minutes from State Street and ten from the academic buildings is worth it. If you decide to be one of these people, you are looking to pay anywhere from $500–$1,000 per month. However, if you can handle taking the city bus, or even doubling that distance to campus, rent prices will drop dramatically. For those unable to pay the higher rates, try housing near Capital Square, notably Carroll Street and Main Street. Housing in these areas are comparable in size to the closer locales and won't charge astronomical amounts.

In general, students are big fans of off-campus housing. Not only do you finally have a place of your own, but you also don't have to travel far from campus. Namely, the areas surrounding State Street and Capital Square are filled with affordable and comfortable housing. Students do advise that you start looking early to secure just the right place.

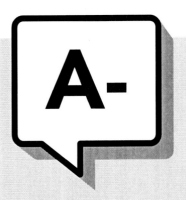

The College Prowler® Grade on

Off-Campus Housing: A-

A high grade in Off-Campus Housing indicates that apartments are of high quality, close to campus, affordable, and easy to secure.

Diversity

The Lowdown On...
Diversity

Native American:
Less than 1%

Asian American:
5%

African American:
2%

Hispanic:
3%

White:
86%

International:
3%

Out-of-State:
29%

Political Activity

Due to the University's liberal nature, UW and political activity share a long and colorful history. Since the school's opening, students have been notorious for forming political rallies and protests. Of course, certain eras in history, like WWII and the Vietnam War, created more student demonstrations than others. There are several student organizations on campus like the College Republicans, Africa without Borders, the Central Asia Student Association, and the European Union Club.

Gay Pride

There is a high acceptance for those who are lesbian, gay, bi-sexual, and transgender. LBGT is an organization geared specifically towards this student population. They hold information fairs, dances, and activity nights, as well as offering counseling services and support groups to students.

Economic Status

While students' financial backgrounds are as varied as the students themselves, a majority of people do come from middle- to upper-class families. Even so, many students depend on loans, government aid, part-time jobs, and scholarships to lessen the financial burdens of college expenses.

Minority Clubs

Student organizations exist everywhere at UW and for almost any cause. Notably, 150 of those groups fall into the culture/ethnic category. There are groups for those who want to share their love of hip-hop, to those of Middle Eastern descent. The Multicultural Student Coalition is one of the more prominent groups on campus. They offer informational fairs, guest speakers, educational forums, and have massed a large student base. However, many of these clubs do not spend much time recruiting others. In the end, it is really up to the individual to find their cause or club.

Most Popular Religions

It's hard to say that any one religion is more 'popular' than another. The student population is filled with those who are Lutheran, Catholic, Jewish, non-denominational, and anything else you can imagine. As a result, there are worshipping facilities for almost every religious sect.

Students Speak Out On...
Diversity

> "It's very diverse. There are lots of Midwesterners, East Coasters, Asians, African Americans, and so on. I love the fact that, in the middle of Wisconsin, you have people from every walk of life."

Q "**It is predominantly white**—but, hey, it's Wisconsin, after all! Compared to my Chicago suburban high school, it is not as diverse. However, you will find people of color on campus and international students. There is a big push towards multiculturalism on this campus."

Q "It's very diverse in terms of personality and different types of people, **but not so much diverse culturally**."

Q "The campus isn't very diverse, but it makes an effort to be. If you aren't white, **you won't be the only person of your minority**, but there is definitely a majority of Caucasian students."

Q "In terms of diversity, Madison is awesome. **About 70 percent of the students are from in state**, so it has a state-school feel. It also represents people from almost everywhere."

Q "**There's always some article in the paper which says that the campus isn't very diverse**, which is sad because they do a lot here to try to attract minority students. There are scholarships for minorities, and minority groups everywhere."

Q "Considering I'm a minority and attend Madison, I'm going to tell you right now that the campus isn't that diverse. I have a strong opinion concerning diversity, and **it seems that at Madison, everyone wants to complain about the lack of diversity**. Both people of color and people not of color complain, but not a whole lot of people make an effort to branch out and hang out with people not like themselves."

Q "The campus is diverse in that people come from all over and their personal beliefs vary, but **racially, there isn't much diversity.**"

Q "**Madison is a liberal campus**, and you'll find there is a lot of acceptance of different ideas and ways of life. As far as race is concerned, it is a pretty white campus. But then again, so is the state of Wisconsin. I really do wish there were more African Americans on campus, but it's not a racist campus by any means. Everyone gets along, and there are lots of clubs and societies set up to help diversify the university."

Q "**The campus is socially, if not racially, diverse**. There are numerous groups of people, and it is possible for any sort of student to find his/her niche in a social group."

Q "The campus somewhat lacks diversity, but can you blame it? **It's in Wisconsin**."

Q "**This campus initially looks about as diverse as a loaf of Wonder Bread**, but when you look around and make some friends, this place is more diverse than most people initially think."

The College Prowler Take On...
Diversity

When it comes to campus diversity, for students, it's more about how you define the term diversity. For those addressing differing personality and lifestyles, Madison is the leader of diversity. This is partly the result of campus-size. With over 45,000 students and hundreds of academic programs, people with every type of quirky element are drawn to UW. More so, many different organizations and clubs are set up to foster and nurture such contrasting people.

Racially, though, UW is not very diverse, as less than 10 percent of the student population falls into minority categories. Many students find this statistic unfortunate, and link it to the university's Midwest location. However, students generally do not downplay the minority population UW does have. Though it may be small, it is very strong in terms of presence. Many of the diversity clubs at the university are the ones offering the most activities and opportunities to students. These clubs will often hold information fairs, social gatherings, debate forums, and educational seminars. One downside is that students don't feel minority groups spend much time on recruitment.

The College Prowler® Grade on

Diversity: D+

A high grade in Diversity indicates that ethnic minorities and international students have a notable presence on campus and that students of different economic backgrounds, religious beliefs, and sexual preferences are well-represented.

Guys & Girls

The Lowdown On...
Guys & Girls

Men Undergrads:
46%

Women Undergrads:
54%

Social Scene

In general, students at UW are very outgoing. If you are at a house party or Greek social, you are sure to find someone to talk with. The bars are the same way, because students here like to party, and with that comes major socialization. UW students will find almost any reason to throw a party or gathering. For those attending the festivities, it means tons of opportunities to meet new and interesting people.

Birth Control Available?

Yes, UW has hormonal contraceptives, birth control pills (list of brands available at the pharmacy, the patch (Ortho Evra), the vaginal ring (NuvaRing), emergency contraceptive pills, Iijectables, Depo-Provera, intrauterine devices, ParaGard Mirena, diaphragm, cervical cap, spermicides, condoms, natural family-planning (fertility-awareness method)

Most Prevalent STDs on Campus

Chlamydia, Gonorrhea, Herpes

Hookups or Relationships?

With a campus the size of an average Midwestern city, there isn't one standard of living when it comes to the opposite sex. Therefore, it is hard to categorize UW as a strictly one-night fling or lasting-love type of school. One common factor, however, is the level of maturity that is associated with such interactions. It seems that those choosing to engage in short-lived romances are pretty levelheaded about it, and understand what's expected and what's not. Similarly, those in serious relationships are relaxed and not too overbearing. Having stated that, there are some stereotypes associated with certain groups of people. The Greek System, for example, is believed to be filled with an endless supply of hormones and little emotional attachment. Also, certain dorms are noted as being more promising to those looking for a quick fix. It is really up to the individual to make their coed experience at Madison what they want it to be.

Best Place to Meet Guys/Girls

In general, the dorms and classrooms are the best places to meet members of the opposite sex. First, they're guaranteed to be at these places. Second, the people you do happen to find have at least one thing in common—they either live in the same dorm or are taking the same class. More so, these commonalties are great neutral topics to start a discussion, which will hopefully lead to more. For those not living in dorms or tired of hitting on classmates, try the bars on the weekends. These establishments are filled with tons of people looking for the same thing you are.

Did You Know?

Top Places to Find Hotties:
1. Helen C. White Library
2. Langdon Street
3. State Street

Top Places to Hook Up:
1. Lakeshore path
2. Dormitories
3. Fraternities and sororities
4. Memorial Library study cubicles

Dress Code

UW itself does not enforce any type of dress code per se. Obviously students are expected to come dressed to class, and decently at that. What one wears really depends on mood and occasion. For 8:50 a.m. lectures, you are sure to find a room filled with pajama pants and UW sweatshirts. If it's a Friday or Saturday night on State St.reet, though, girls and guys will be in their party wear. For the girls, it's usually tight black pants or jeans and figure-fitting tops. For the guys, it's clean jeans, a buttoned down shirt, or a soft sweater. Any other time of the day, it is really up to you to choose your apparel and style.

Students Speak Out On...
Guys & Girls

"Madison is a beautiful town—everyone I meet is attractive. Everyone is very friendly and down-to-earth for the most part. You can meet people easily, and most people smile at you on the street!"

Q "Everyone wants to meet people. **The students are really friendly**, and I'm sure you'll make close friends quickly."

Q "Well, as a guy, I was in heaven. **I had fun—let's put it that way.**"

Q "**Some guys are hot, some are ugly**. It is the same with the girls. I met my boyfriend here, so maybe you'll meet one, too."

Q "Most of these people are from the Midwest—Wisconsin, Minnesota, or Illinois—so if I were to group all the people, it would be a Midwestern mentality. Most people are very nice, but **you always have those jerks that are full of themselves.**"

Q "**They are hot**! I mean come on now—there's 40,000 students, so you have a whole range to choose from!"

Q "There is a large selection to chose from at Wisconsin. The girls are very pretty and the guys are really hot. I have never had a problem on the guy front for sure! **Plenty of eye candy here.**"

Q "I can't really say about the guys, **but the girls are gorgeous**."

Q "The guys are hot! But of course, many of them are players, so be careful! In general, they are really nice, and you meet a lot of cool guys. The girls, on the other hand, tend to be catty. Since I'm from the Midwest, I see a drastic difference between Midwestern girls and East Coast girls. The coasties are annoying, but it makes Madison more diverse, so you'll learn to deal. Don't worry, though, because you'll meet tons of great friends. The people at Madison are really nice; **you definitely feel the Madison hospitality**."

Q "Everyone's hot here! **Just come to Chi Phi, and we'll show you a good time**."

Q "It's hard to walk to class here without checking out at least a dozen people in this town. Most of the people you'll meet are Thursday through Saturday partiers, and Sunday through Wednesday studiers. **It's all about trying to juggle work and play at this school**. You have to do both."

The College Prowler Take On...
Guys & Girls

Students agree that the student body is very eye pleasing, literally. While there is a little more commentary about the girls, they do not discount the attractiveness of the male population. Looks aside, students do find most people to be accepting and friendly in nature. This "Midwestern mentality" makes it easy for new students or visors to feel comfortable at UW.

UW brings a wide range of people, and with that comes a wide range of personalities. It's not really fair to typify the guys into one group and the girls into another. Overall, there are a lot of friendly people. Whether you're in class, at work, or at a party, it is very easy to find someone to chat with, and more so to feel comfortable in your surroundings. That is the key—to find the environment you're into. On the flip side, you will find those that you clash with. Class-wise, this is great because it creates dialogue and debate, and hopefully both sides will leave the conversation with a better understanding of each other. Socially, this can be a problem, but only if you let it. Know whom you can and cannot tolerate outside of the classroom, and choose your social events accordingly.

The College Prowler® Grade on
Guys: B+

A high grade for Guys indicates that the male population on campus is attractive, smart, friendly, and engaging, and that the school has a decent ratio of guys to girls.

The College Prowler® Grade on
Girls: A-

A high grade for Girls not only implies that the women on campus are attractive, smart, friendly, and engaging, but also that there is a fair ratio of girls to guys.

Athletics

The Lowdown On...
Athletics

Athletic Division:
NCAA Division I

Conference:
Big Ten

School Mascot
Bucky the Badger

Males Playing Varsity Sports:
372 (3%)

Females Playing Varsity Sports:
387 (3%)

➔

Men's Varsity Sports:

Basketball
Cross-Country
Football
Golf
Hockey
Rowing
Soccer
Swimming
Tennis
Track & Field
Wrestling

Women's Varsity Sports:

Basketball
Cross-Country
Golf
Hockey
Rowing (Openweight
and Lightweight)
Soccer
Softball
Swimming
Tennis
Track & Field
Volleyball

Intramurals:

Basketball
Flag Football
Floor Hockey
Ice Hockey
Soccer

(Intramurals, continued)
Softball
Volleyball
Sand Volleyball
Tennis
Ultimate Frisbee

Club Sports:

Aikido
Archery
Badminton
Baseball
Capoeira
Chinese Wu Shu
Cycling
Dance Team
Eagle Claw Kung Fu
Fencing
Figure Skating
Frisbee
Ice Hockey
Japanese Karate
Kendo
Lacrosse
Racquetball
Rugby
Running
Shorin Ryu Karate
Squash
Tae Kwon Do
Triathlon
Volleyball
Water Polo
Water Skiing & Wakeboarding

Athletic Fields

Nine softball diamonds, two rugby pitches, ten sand volleyball courts, four lighted football fields, two lacrosse fields, six soccer fields, one ultimate Frisbee field, fifteen half-court basketball courts, twenty-four outdoor tennis courts

Getting Tickets

Getting tickets depends on the sport and the competition. Football games are very popular, and many students buy season tickets. If you are only looking to attend a few weekend games, it's easiest just to find someone with season tickets who can't make that weekend's game. Otherwise, just contact the ticketing office for seat availability information.

Wisconsin Athletic Ticket Office
Kohl Center
601 W. Dayton St.
(608) 262-1440 or (800)-462-2343
Fax: (608) 265-4931
tickets@athletics.wisc.edu

Most Popular Sports

Football, basketball, hockey

Overlooked Teams

Rugby, water polo, badminton

Best Place to Take a Walk

Lakeshore Path, State Street, Capital Square

Gyms/Facilities

Lathrop

Natatorium

Nielsen

Porter Boathouse

Shell

Southeast Recreational Facility (SERF)

Students Speak Out On...
Athletics

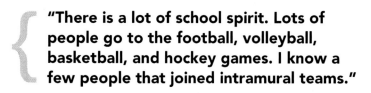

"There is a lot of school spirit. Lots of people go to the football, volleyball, basketball, and hockey games. I know a few people that joined intramural teams."

Q "Sports are huge, **especially hockey and football**. Make sure you go to the games."

Q "**Football is the biggest sport at Wisconsin**, and the games are really fun. Everyone tailgates before the game, and the students get really rowdy. The club sports (non-varsity) are good as well. I am a member of the club lacrosse team, and we travel to places like New Orleans, for a Mardi Gras tournament."

Q "Varsity sports are great. I think Big Ten athletics by far offer the most for the sports fan as well as the competitor. I played intramural football, basketball, hockey, and softball. **Pick-up games are abundant** at the Natatorium, SERF (South East Recreational Facility), and the SHELL, where the athletes work out. Definitely get season tickets for football, basketball, and hockey."

Q "**Varsity sports are huge here**. Football games are some of the best times you will have, and hockey and basketball also have large followings. Intramural sports are a ton of fun to get into, because there are a lot of great athletes who aren't playing varsity sports."

Q "It's a Big Ten school, so **we're very into our sports**, especially football."

Q "Varsity football is big, as you'd guess. Basketball is big. Hockey is big. **Everything else is always available to go see the day of the event**, and I don't think tickets are too bad; the cheapest way is to buy season tickets if you want to see all the games. I play intramural sports a lot. I played soccer for two years, as well as basketball and softball. It's around $10 to play a season, once you split the entry fee up with everyone else on your team."

Q "Intramural sports are cool. I played floor hockey this year. **They're easy to sign up for and lots of fun.**"

Q "Varsity sports are huge. Football, basketball, and hockey are all big. The fans are so fun and the games are great. **Even if you don't like the sport, it's fun to go to the games.**"

Q "Varsity sports at Madison are insane. They might not be the best, but **football dominates the fall**. Basketball and hockey rule the winter and spring. If you can get tickets to the games, get them. It's so much fun and just amazing. You get up in the morning, get a little drunk, and then go to the games. Even if you don't drink, the games are still a lot of fun. The student section is crazy, and it's impossible to not have a good time. Intramurals are a lot of fun, too. There are so many different sports you can do. You will definitely be able to find the one you like."

Q "Football is huge. **Definitely order tickets the day you get the application** or you might not get them, because the upperclassmen get their tickets during the previous school year. They are so much fun to go to. The only other sport worth going to is boys' basketball because we won the Big 10. Intramural sports aren't that big."

Q "**Both varsity and IM sports are huge on campus**. Plan early for either."

Q "Varsity sports on campus are very large, with home football, hockey, and basketball games **playing a large part of not only student, but Madison social life**. IM sports are also popular with those who take the time to seek them out, as they are readily available."

Q "**Varsity sports on campus become a drinking occasion** (much like everything else) and most students partake during football season."

The College Prowler Take On...
Athletics

Nobody denies the intense role athletics play at UW. For Saturday Badger Football games, any number of houses will start the athletic support by throwing parties and getting decked out in Badger wear, complete with body paint and large posters, all before nine a.m. The football stadium has a special student seating section that is crowded with supportive, sometimes intoxicated students. While football is probably the most viewed and attended sport, there are many other athletic events. Intramurals are offered through the athletic department and even different resident halls. IM sports are taken relatively seriously, though viewed more as a social activity than a true athletic event.

Overall, UW does not lack in providing athletic opportunities. For those needing serious and heavy competition, varsity sports are the place to be in. Many of UW's teams are successful and will travel for conference and tournament events. Students wanting something more low-key should check out intramurals. You form your own team and compete against other teams on campus. Lastly, if you're looking for something a little different, check out the club sports. Students can pick-up aikido, figure skating, or wakeboarding.

The College Prowler® Grade on
Athletics: A

A high grade in Athletics indicates that students have school spirit, that sports programs are respected, that games are well-attended, and that intramurals are a prominent part of student life.

Nightlife

The Lowdown On...
Nightlife

Popular Nightlife Spots!
Club Prowler:

Club Inferno
1718 Commercial Ave.
(608) 245-9583
www.clubinferno.com
Club Inferno features many live acts, as well as DJs who spin all sorts of music, from house and jungle, to hip-hop and goth.

The Majestic
115 King St.
(608) 251-2582
The Majestic is one of Madison's few nightclubs; it is close to Capital Square, and many go there for the lush atmosphere and pricey drinks. The music is incredible, and the patrons are usually upperclassmen.

➜

Bar Prowler:

Angelic Brewing Company
322 W Johnson St.
(608) 257-2707
www.angelicbrewing.com
Located minutes from State Street, this heaven-themed restaurant is perfect for an evening with friends or visiting family. Inside there is a bar, jukebox, pool tables, and dart boards.

Blue Velvet Lounge
430 W Gilman St.
(608) 250-9900
Voted for "best cocktails" by UW's student paper, this lounge creates a trendy atmosphere with cushy seats and low lighting. Friday and Saturday nights are the busiest for this up-scale lounge. Drop in and try their famous cosmopolitan and strawberry champagne cocktail.

Brothers
704 University Ave.
(608) 251-9550
Brothers is a typical college bar with lots of fashionably-clad students grinding to the latest hits. If that's your sort of scene, then you should feel right at home.

Bull Feathers
303 N Henry St.
(608) 257-6444
Bull Feathers is suitable for any night and any occasion. Many seek refuge after a long day or just to catch up with friends. The drinks are reasonable and there's a welcoming crowd. If you're heading here on a weekend, be prepared for a long wait.

The Kollege Klub
529 N Lake St.
(608) 257-3611
Known as "the KK," this large bar is a magnet for frat boys, freshmen, and athletes. Drinks aren't all that expensive, and the crowd is pretty decent. Students say you have to go there at least once to truly complete the UW undergrad experience.

Nitty Gritty Restaurant and Bar
223 N Frances St.
(608) 251-2521
This place is essential for birthdays. Customers on their special day receive free drinks, a nitty gritty mug, and obnoxious waiters. If it's your 21st though, be prepared for excessive treatment and attention. Students must go for at least one birthday.

Paul's Club
212 State St.
(608) 257-5250
This is one of State Street's nicer bars. Inside, there is comfortable seating, attractive lighting, jukeboxes, and a large fake tree. There can sometimes be a line, but for this place it is worth it.

State Street Brats
603 State St.
(608) 255-5544
www.statestreetbrats.com
Founded in 1932, State Street Brats is the original creator of the red (smoked) brat. The second floor has stadium seating and two 10 foot screens for watching the game on weekends.

Other Places to Check Out:
The Barrymore Theater
The Church Key
Genna's Lounge
Kimia Lounge
Opus Lounge
The Orpheum Theater
The Paradise
The Plaza Tavern
Porta Bella Wine Cellar
The State Bar & Grill

Bars Close At:
2 a.m.

Primary Areas with Nightlife:
State Street
Capital Square
Memorial Union
Union Terrace

Cheapest Place to Get a Drink:
The Kollege Klub
State Street Brats

Favorite Drinking Games:
Beer Pong
Card Games (A$$hole)
Century Club
Quarters
Power Hour

Student Favorites:
Bar hopping
Going out to eat
Greek parties
House parties
Live shows
Union events

Useful Resources for Nightlife

Pick up a copy of the *Isthmus*. This Madison-based newspaper lists all the social events for the upcoming weekend. You can find information on new movies, touring acts, and coffeehouse shows.

What to Do if You're Not 21

If you aren't of age, or simply don't want to go to the bars, check out "Today at the Union." This is a listing of all the day's events at both unions, and you are sure to find a show or free event occurring. One of the more popular union events is "Free Art Nights." On the weekends students have complete access to pottery wheels, loose clay, and collage materials. There is no fee for this event, and students can even get their pottery pieces glazed and fired. Open mic nights are also frequent in Madison, and the local coffee houses or lounges will usually host them.

Organization Parties

Many of the student organizations at UW will house parties for their members, or to gain more members. These are usually held at the Union or somebody's apartment. Other organizations like the Ten Percent Society simply sponsor parties where anyone and everyone is welcomed to attend.

Frats

See the Greek section!

Students Speak Out On...
Nightlife

> **"Socially, the school rocks. Whether you prefer house parties, bars, or frats, you have tons of options. I never get bored. I always look forward to finishing my week so I can live it up on the weekends."**

Q "Bars on State Street are plentiful. We actually sometimes got so tired of them all that we'd often pick a road on a map going out of town and **just drive, stopping at all the bars along the way**. My favorite bar is Joe Hart's, which is now called Brothers."

Q "I really do not hang out way off campus. I like to hang out **on campus on State Street or near the capital**. The bars are a lot of fun! Clubs in Madison—well, I don't think you can really go clubbing in Madison."

Q "**The bar scene in Madison is like no other**. It is awesome. I can tell you all about it, but you really have to experience a weekend here to understand it. There are about 40 on-campus bars, and as an underclassman, it's not hard to get into them."

Q "I don't really know because I don't drink. But **I wish there were a few more places where you could see bands on this campus**. There are a few good bars, I know, because I have friends who like hanging out there."

Q "There are so many bars, **you would definitely need a fake ID**. I like going to the KK and the State, though there are so many fun bars. Madison definitely doesn't lack things to do for fun."

Q "**Unfortunately, Madison has no good clubs**, but there's always parties and some bars that play good music to dance too. But one cool fact is that Madison's Union still serves beer. Sitting on the terrace in the spring with a beer is nice. UW-Madison is definitely cool."

Q "**The bar scene is good in Madison**. Wisconsin has the highest ratio of bars to people, and pretty much everyone likes to drink. If you have a fake ID, assuming that you are under 21, there are lots of places you can go."

Q "I hear the bar and club scene is pretty good in Madison. I didn't get my fake in time to check out the bars, but Madison is one of the best party schools in the nation. **The police are cracking down more on underage kids** in bars, but just get a good fake and you'll be alright."

Q "Most of the bars are 21-and-up, and to get into them you will need a fake ID. **People head down to State Street to frequent the bars Tuesday through Saturday**. There aren't many clubs on campus, which sucks, but Madison is much more of a bar type of a place. Don't go to Brothers if your ID isn't really good because they take them away there."

Q "On any given night, there is always a party you can get into. Some are less fun than others, but they're always big, loud, and filled with people. **If you want to get into the party scene, all you have to do is make friends**. Invitations will roll in."

Q "State Street, along with good restaurants, is where most of the bars are. I like the Church Key (a church turned bar) and the Kollege Klub. The Memorial Union, which sits on the lake, serves beer in movie theater popcorn buckets! The bars and clubs in Madison are all really cool, and vary in style and atmosphere—I'm sure **you'll find your niche**."

Q "The house parties vary, they are all crowded, but some of them (where no one does anything but stand shoulder to shoulder and push at the beer line) suck, and some of them (like the ones after a football game where everyone is hopefully in a good mood) rock. Not going to reveal the "good" spots, most of my secret places don't need a bigger crowd. But lots of people go to Brats, Brothers, and if you want to **get the most drunk for your buck**, hit up the Kollege Klub!"

Q "Parties are always going on, but they are usually overcrowded house parties. **The bar scene is also good, but no clubs worth going to.**"

Q "As a freshman, most parties will be a random house party—sweaty, crowded, loud, and essential to the first year experience. Afterwards, **parties will occur at the apartments or houses of friends**, and will usually lead to the bars. The atmospheres of bars in Madison range from the essential college bars (KK, Brats, Brothers), to somewhat more relaxed bars consisting of older crowds (Genna's, Paul's Club), to swank bars such as those around the capital."

Q "**The bars in Madison are great**. If you want to hit up a dive where you'll always run into someone you know, go to the Plaza on Henry Street, or the Paradise by the capital. Paul's Club on State has a great atmosphere, and so do the Opus and the Kimia Lounge up by the capital. If you like wine, go to Porta Bella Wine Cellar just off State."

The College Prowler Take On...
Nightlife

For weekend activities, it's really about what students are in the mood for and what's accessible. Due to the closeness of State Street and its insane amount of bars, students do often find themselves at these locations. For those unfamiliar with the bar scene, students suggest popular places like the KK. If bars aren't your thing, then house parties are another popular option. However, there are a lot of things to do that don't include alcohol and heavy crowds. Students find just as much entertainment in Madison's comedy clubs, coffee shops, or the live band performances.

UW definitely has a reputation for being a party school, and the majority of students fulfill this image. Going to the bars on State Street or to house parties are by far the most popular options when it comes to Madison's nightlife. Those wanting something else, though, should not despair. Also on State Street are a few performing art centers where students can take in a play or musical. Madison's Civic Center attracts touring acts like Rent, Chicago, and The Nutcracker Ballet. Here students can also take in touring musicians like John Mayer and Pete Yorn. There are also UW sponsored events like samba lessons, yoga instruction, and photography classes to partake in. In the end it's simply matter of deciding how you want to spend your precious weekend time.

A

The College Prowler® Grade on
Nightlife: A

A high grade in Nightlife indicates that there are many bars and clubs in the area that are easily accessible and affordable. Other determining factors include the number of options for the under-21 crowd and the prevalence of house parties.

Greek Life

The Lowdown On...
Greek Life

Number of Fraternities:
26

Number of Sororities:
14

Undergrad Men in Fraternities:
9%

Undergrad Women in Sororities:
8%

Fraternities:

Acacia
Alpha Delta Phi
Alpha Epsilon Pi
Alpha Gamma Rho
Beta Theta Pi
Chi Phi
Chi Psi
Delta Tau Delta
Delta Theta Sigma
Delta Upsilon
Kappa Sigma
Phi Beta Sigma
Phi Delta Theta
Phi Kappa Tau
Pi Lambda Phi
Sigma Alpha Epsilon
Sigma Alpha Mu
Sigma Chi
Sigma Phi
Sigma Phi Epsilon
Sigma Pi
Tau Kappa Epsilon
Theta Delta Chi
Triangle
Zeta Beta Tau
Zeta Psi

Sororities:

Alpha Chi Omega
Alpha Epsilon Phi
Alpha Kappa Alpha
Alpha Phi
Alpha Pi Omega
Chi Omega
Delta Delta Delta
Delta Gamma
Gamma Phi Beta
Kappa Alpha Theta
Kappa Kappa Gamma
Pi Beta Phi
Sigma Delta Tau
Sigma Lambda Gamma

Multicultural Colonies:

Alpha Phi Alpha, Fraternity
Delta Sigma Theta, Sorority
Lambda Theta Alpha, Sorority
Omega Psi Phi, Fraternity
Zeta Phi Beta, Sorority

Other Greek Organizations:

Panhellenic Association
Interfraternity Council
All-Greek Council
National Panhellenic Council

Did You Know?

An average of **10 percent of the undergraduate population is a member of the Greek system**. This statistic holds true for the freshman population as well.

The Greek system was set in place only a few years after the university opened, making it **one of the oldest established systems associated with UW**.

Apart from house parties, the **societies do host fundraising, intramural sporting, and academic events**.

Students Speak Out On...
Greek Life

{ **"Greek life doesn't dominate at all. If you choose to join, that is cool and fun, and if not, you are no better off. It is great either way. It just depends on what you want."**

Q "Greek life makes up about 10 percent of the school population, but that's really not a lot at Madison. **Wisconsin isn't a school where you need to go Greek to be social.** I was in a sorority, but I'm planning on dropping it, because I realized how I don't need it. It's just good to rush a house because you meet people that way."

Q "**I was Greek there, and I didn't think that it dominated the social scene.** If you let it though, it will. It helps to spend time away from your fraternity so you aren't always surrounded by it. Definitely rush—Greek Week is a blast every year. Then again, it is all what you make of it."

Q "I don't think that Greek life dominates the social scene. **Some people are into that stuff and others aren't.** I'm not in a sorority, but I know a couple people who are, and I have been able to enjoy a few frat parties without having to join one of those organizations."

Q "Greek life only represents 10 percent of the total student population, so that's 4,000 out of 40,000. It does not dominate the social scene. **I do not think it is necessary to be involved in Greek life to have fun** at Madison. I am not in a sorority, and I don't regret it one bit!"

Q "Greek life is big on campus if you're in it, but otherwise it doesn't matter. **Most people aren't a part of the Greek system** here, and you don't need it to have fun."

Q "Greeks do not dominate. **They are there if you want them, but can be avoided**. There's a specific part of campus where all of the houses are, so if you don't want anything to do with them, just don't hang around that part."

Q "Greek life is huge. You'll have many choices, but Greek life doesn't rule the campus at all. There's always something going on. **House parties are everywhere**."

Q "The Greek life is not that big. **I am in a sorority and I love it, but it is not necessary at all**. It is being forced to become dry so the parties have to be held in bars, and then it is harder to get in. It is a good way to meet friends and get involved in other campus activities."

Q "Langdon Street is where most of the frat houses are, and although many people belong to Greek clubs, it does not, by far, dominate the school. I lived one block from Langdon this year, but I never felt as if they were everywhere. I don't belong to a sorority, but I know people who do, and it's a pretty chill scene. There is a **diverse student body at UW** consisting of hippies, Greeks, some punks, sporty kids, and foreign students, but the main thing in common is that everyone likes to party!"

Q "Greek life is loud and shiny. **Most people's first few parties up here are at frats**. Unless you want to join a frat or a sorority or have friends in them, it's very easy to find social scenes where Greek life is barely present. I'm really not kidding when I say you can find a group of people for just about anything you want or are interested in at this place."

Q "Greek life is fun, probably because I'm in a sorority. I'm in Delta Delta Delta and I love it, love it, love it. About 10 percent of students are in the Greek system. Depending on where you live freshman year, you will see more or less Greeks. If you live in University housing, you will probably go to more house parties than frats because of the longer walk. If **you live in private housing, you go to more parties at the frats**. I lived at the Langdon on Langdon Street, which is where most of their houses are. I love the Greek system, and I recommend at least checking it out if you are somewhat interested."

Q "The Greek life isn't that big, **but they do make a lot of noise**."

Q "Greek life does not dominate the social scene. However, if you choose to become part of the Greek system, **it may come to dominate your social scene**. Once in the Greek system, most of those in sororities or fraternities end up spending large amounts of social time with others in fraternities and sororities."

Q "I wouldn't say it dominates the scene, but **it's definitely here to stay**."

The College Prowler Take On...
Greek Life

While Greek life is alive and thriving at UW, it is not a dominating life force. Most of the students affected by the Greek system are members of a fraternity or sorority. For these students, the lifestyle of the Greek can be a little overwhelming. If nothing else, students feel their experience in this system has helped them meet a lot of interesting people. While the sororities and fraternities do offer plenty of socialization, students don't feel it is the only way to meet people at UW.

UW is home to nearly forty sororities and fraternities. While some are geared towards its members being of a certain ethnicity or academic field, they all offer a strong social aspect. Those in the Greek system often partake in intramural events, fundraising nights, and volunteer activities. Furthermore, the Greek System is not totally exclusive. Even if students are not a part of a frat or sorority, they are usually welcome at most of their parties or other social events.

The College Prowler® Grade on
Greek Life: A-

A high grade in Greek Life indicates that sororities and fraternities are not only present, but also active on campus. Other determining factors include the variety of houses available and the respect the Greek community receives from the rest of the campus.

Drug Scene

The Lowdown On...
Drug Scene

Most Prevalent Drugs on Campus:

Alcohol

Marijuana

Liquor-Related Referrals:

119

Liquor-Related Arrests:

882

Drug-Related Referrals:

47

Drug-Related Arrests:

166

Drug Counseling Programs

Alcohol Smart Classes

(608) 222-7311

UHS Counseling

905 University Ave.

Monday, Tuesday, Thursday, Friday 8:30 a.m.–5 p.m., Wednesday 9 a.m.–5 p.m.

(608) 265-5600

Student Health/Mental Health Services

881 Commonwealth Ave. (west entrance)

(617) 353-3575

Students Speak Out On...
Drug Scene

> "Drugs are pretty easy to obtain at Madison, especially pot. You can smell people smoking it during most house parties and often at night."

Q "**Drugs are very prevalent**, depending on the crowd you hang out with. It's up to you—if you want it you can find it, if you don't it won't come find you."

Q "Naturally drugs are prevalent at basically every school you go to, but **it is not an issue if you don't want it to be**."

Q "**I saw a lot of drug use at parties** and it is there, but it really depends on the crowd you hang out with."

Q "**Drugs are prevalent, but not overwhelming**. You can avoid it if you want, but you can also participate easily."

Q "**Drugs do exist at Madison, but you don't have to partake in them**. Mainly, people just smoke weed, but I do have friends who do worse. Like any city and any campus, you always have the hardcore drugs, but they are definitely avoidable. Be careful at frat parties with drugs like roofies. I got drugged last year and had to go to detox. It was super scary so watch yourself, whether you go to Madison or any other campus. Roofies exist. Don't think that it can't happen to you, because it can."

Q "Not many drugs at all. **I haven't really seen that much besides pot**."

Q "There are drugs around, but it is all about **who you hang out with**."

Q "**There is a decent amount of weed smoking**, but it depends on who you hang around with. You can do it or you can avoid it."

Q "Drugs are pretty big here. There's tons of weed, and then probably a bit of everything else—cocaine, shrooms, and **a lot of pharmaceutical abuse** (Ritalin, Adderall, and any pain-killer you can get). This is not to say that everyone is on drugs, because most aren't."

Q "I know of prescription drug abuse, cokeheads, and marijuana use, but **none of it is forced on anyone**. Or at least I haven't experienced that."

Q "If you go here, you're going to meet people who do drugs. If you want, you'll find out how to get them. If this bothers you, it's easy to ignore these people and this scene, but **if you're social, you will run into it**. The guys in the drug scene are usually well-educated and laid-back, so you're not going to be bothered by them if you want nothing to do with them."

The College Prowler Take On...
Drug Scene

Students do not deny the presence and habitual use of drugs at UW. Whether it is alcohol, marijuana, or prescription pills, many have seen or experienced drug use first-hand. The easiest drugs to obtain are alcohol and marijuana. Students say that house parties and dorms are some of the easiest places to obtain these drugs.

The choice to use drugs is really just that—a choice. Students don't feel pressured to do drugs, and say the amount of drugs being used generally depends on the crowd with which you associate. If the campus or Madison police catch you with illegal substances, there will be consequences. Officers don't think twice about handing out tickets along with hefty fines.

The College Prowler® Grade on

Drug Scene: C+

A high grade in the Drug Scene indicates that drugs are not a noticeable part of campus life; drug use is not visible, and no pressure to use them seems to exist.

Campus Strictness

The Lowdown On...
Campus Strictness

What Are You Most Likely to Get Caught Doing on Campus?
- Underage drinking
- Using a fake ID
- Fighting in bars
- Plagiarizing

Students Speak Out On...
Campus Strictness

> "Police on campus are awesome, so long as you are under control. They will occasionally go into bars and give out tickets to scare people, but I've shared a beer with a cop on a few occasions."

Q "Watch out for the Campus Police. **They are very visible.** They will bust you at the bars for having a fake ID, so be careful!"

Q "The cops are annoying about alcohol if you are underage, **although most bars are easy to get into**."

Q "Drinking on any campus is going to happen. It is how smart you are about it. **I had a fake ID the entire time I wasn't 21, and I never got caught**. I didn't get overly drunk in a bar when I was underage—all you do is highlight yourself. It is harder now with computerized IDs. The city cops infiltrate the bars now and then to card people. The campus police aren't too big into busting parties because the city cops do it all."

Q "The city cops get annual funding for a program called Operation Sting, where they have young-looking cops go undercover to bust house parties. That sucks for the people renting the house, but for the party-goers, it wasn't a big deal—**they usually just let you go**."

Q "The police turn the other cheek for the most part about drinking. The vast majority of people do it on this campus. Odds are you won't get busted with drugs, either, if **you're smart about it**."

Q "Campus police don't bother students. If you're at a party that gets busted, **they just make you dump out your cup and leave**. Usually only the house owners get a ticket. If you're not stupid about drinking, you won't get caught. Don't carry your cup from party to party. Don't smoke weed in the dorms, you'll get a write-up. They say two write ups and you get kicked out, but I think it's negotiable."

Q "Sometimes you'll get fake ID tickets at the bars. It's not strict besides that. We had a huge block party where **everyone was drinking all over the streets** and the cops didn't do a thing. They even posed for pictures where they pretended to put people in handcuffs."

Q "The police are pretty laid-back on drinking and drugs. As long as you control yourself, the cops don't really mind. If the cops bust a party, the only people who get in trouble are the people having the party. They let everybody else leave. In fact, the last week of school in the spring there is a street party. Every house on each side of the street for about four blocks has a party starting at noon on the same day. They set their kegs outside and everyone drinks. The cops stand around, and as long as you don't start vandalizing or making an idiot of yourself, **they let you have your fun**."

Q "The cops are annoying. They are always in the bars checking IDs so be careful. I got caught and received a $345 ticket for being underage in a bar. **For the most part, they don't bother you**."

Q "Every year, there is a Mifflin block party on Cinco de Mayo. Last year, there were at least 5,000 kids drinking and each house probably had about 20 kegs. There were about 40 cops there, and they were all watching us get plastered! They were super cool about it and there to make sure no fights or riots broke out. **That's pretty lenient if you ask me**."

Q "I've never had any run-ins with police about drinking or drugs. **But then again, I've never done anything ridiculously stupid**. Don't spend too much time at college-crowd bars with a fake."

Q "If you are smart and don't get too wasted, they are pretty forgiving. However, if you fall in Lake Monona after a long night out in February, and break into the Monona Terrace, **they are a little more strict**—not that I would know anything about that—at least I don't remember."

Q "**The police here tend to go for the source while leaving individuals alone**. You'll see large, loud parties getting busted, and when that happens, the people supplying the alcohol get the fines, while most of the drinkers get away. When it comes to drugs, cops aim for the dealers instead of the buyers."

The College Prowler Take On...
Campus Strictness

Campus Police tend to have a relaxed reign over the student population. As a result, there isn't a sense of strictness on campus. Bar and house parties are the most common places police will be interacting with students. Campus Police will come down on underage drinking and the use of fake IDs. Apart from that, though, students feel free and able to do what they choose.

As long as you use some amount of common sense or discretion, you really won't have any problems with Campus Police or strictness. However, those who decide to drink underage at a loud party will run the chance of getting busted and then fined. Similarly, if you're caught using a fake ID, consequences await you. In terms of academics, the campus is rigid. They follow the 'zero tolerance' rule that only allows you one act of academic dishonesty. After being caught, you are expelled, and the offense stays on your academic record. Weigh every option and the potential consequences before deciding to do something potentially illegal.

The College Prowler® Grade on
Campus
Strictness: A

A high Campus Strictness grade implies an overall lenient atmosphere; police and RAs are fairly tolerant, and the administration's rules are flexible.

Parking

The Lowdown On...
Parking

Approximate Parking Permit Cost:

$50–$120 per month

Freshmen Allowed to Park?

Yes

Student Parking Lot?

Offered by various dorms

Common Parking Tickets:

Expired Meter: $10,
$60 if towed

No Parking Zone: $25,
$75 if towed

Fire Lane: $50,
$100 if towed

Handicapped Zone: $100,
$150 if towed

Parking Permits

Students are sometimes able to purchase permits through the dormitory they are living in. Otherwise, real estate agencies like Steve Brown and Isthmus apartments offer parking spots in their various lots.

UW Parking Services

UW does offer parking permits to students apart from the space the dorms provide. Students must submit an application, and the sooner they do the better. Parking spaces are assigned mid-August for the upcoming year. Don't be surprised if you are not awarded a spot, though. Those wishing to contest can fill out an appeal form, but again don't get your hopes up.

Did You Know?

Best Places to Find a Parking Spot

Wisconsin Avenue

Gilman Street pay lots

State Sreet parking ramp

Good Luck Getting a Parking Spot Here!

Langdon Street

Carroll Street

Park Street

Randall Street

Students Speak Out On...
Parking

{ "Don't bring a car. Everything is within walking distance. Once you have an apartment in your later years, you'll also have a parking spot, so it won't be a problem to bring a car if you want one."

Q "**Parking is a nightmare**. You can park if you have a permit while in the dorms, but they are expensive. If you choose to live off campus, I would bring a car. City permits are inexpensive, so parking on the streets isn't too bad. Most apartment complexes have underground parking or lots for a fee as well."

Q "Parking is horrible on campus! **Do not bring your car, especially if you live in the dorms**, because there is nowhere to park. When you are a freshman, it isn't necessary to bring your car."

Q "Parking is terrible on campus. Unless you have a spot, which can cost up to $100 a month, don't expect to find a place to park. **You can't drive to class**, either, and it's more fun to walk anyway."

Q "**Parking is a little ridiculous**, but people usually don't drive to class. You can get a spot somewhere, but they are expensive."

Q "This is the worst place to find a parking spot in the world. Parking is terrible. Everyone here has mopeds. I swear, **this is the moped capital of the world**."

Q "**Parking is difficult as a freshman**, and even for upperclassmen, but I think you will find that everything you need is within walking distance so there is no need for a car."

Q "Parking is minimal. I don't have a car so I don't really know first-hand. There is parking available, but you may have to pay a monthly fee. I would recommend not bringing one. If you live on campus or downtown you really don't need one. **Bring a bike—Madison is super bike friendly**, and it is the easiest way to get around. I walk and bike everywhere."

Q "Parking is terrible. You can't drive to classes because there is no parking. **Many students have mopeds**. Madison is a huge moped campus. I definitely want one, but it isn't necessary, because there is a free bus that takes you to buildings on campus."

Q "Parking is expensive, and if you get a residential parking pass, parking spaces are scarce and cars need to be moved every two or three days. In addition, when it snows, certain sides of the street are blocked. Either **share parking spot costs with roommates**, or be a bum and borrow cars."

Q "**Parking in Madison is a nightmare**. Unless you're renting a space, good luck finding one at night. And if you are renting one, you're paying anywhere from $60–$100 a month for it. For parking your car over night, I recommend the huge parking facilities set up all over the city. It can be expensive if you leave a car there for too long, but overall it's the easiest way to park."

The College Prowler Take On...
Parking

Students overwhelmingly agree that parking at UW is awful. Whether you're on the streets or in a ramp, finding a spot to leave your car can be frustrating. Students who need a car on campus usually decide to buy a permit. However, your reserved parking spot may be a few blocks away and at a high price. Parking only gets worse during athletic event weekends or on concert nights. Students are rarely able to find a spot during these times. As a result, many students opt to use mopeds rather than cars when traveling about campus.

While the city offers three ramps near campus, it isn't enough to convince students to bring a car to campus. The majority of the time, parking becomes more of a headache than it's worth. Mopeds are more popular because the school is more accommodating to them. Almost every academic building has areas sectioned off for mopeds to park. UW also offers a campus shuttle for those needing to get farther on campus. Overall, students should really take advantage of the various transportation options before deciding to bring a car to UW.

The College Prowler® Grade on

Parking: D

A high grade in this section indicates that parking is both available and affordable, and that parking enforcement isn't overly severe.

Transled

The Lowdown On...
Transportation

Ways to Get Around Town:

On Campus
Bicycle
L-Bus
Moped

Public Transportation
Metro Transit Bus System

Taxi Cabs
Badger Cab
Union Cab

Car Rentals
Alamo
(800) 327-9633
www.alamo.com

Avis
(608) 251-2078
(800) 831-2847
www.avis.com

Budget
(608) 258-3526
(800) 527-0700
www.budget.com

Dollar
(800) 800-4000
www.dollar.com

(Car Rentals, continued)

Enterprise
(800) 736-8222
www.enterprise.com

Hertz
(608) 242-9870
(800) 654-3131
www.hertz.com

National
(800) 227-7368
www.nationalcar.com

Best Ways to Get Around Town

The L-bus is a free transportation service that loops around the campus and can get you from one end to the next in fifteen minutes. For those living off campus, mopeds have become very popular. If you need to get to the mall or somewhere more than twenty minutes away, take a cab. The city bus is an option, but you need to have a lot of time on your hands. The buses make several stops, and before going too deep into town they make a required, lengthy, stop at the transfer station.

Ways to Get Out of Town:

Airport

Dane County Airport
www.co.dane.wi.us/airport
4000 International Ln.
(608) 246-3380

Airlines Serving Madison

ATA
(800) 435-9282
www.ata.com

American Airlines
(800) 433-7300
www.aa.com

Continental
(800) 523-3273
www.continental.com

Delta
(800) 221-1212
www.delta.com

Northwest
(800) 225-2525
www.nwa.com

Midwest Airlines
(800) 452-2022
www.midwestairlines.com

Trans World Express (TWA)
800-221-2000

United
(800) 241-6522
www.united.com

US Airways
(800) 428-4322
www.usairways.com

How to Get to the Airport

Heading north to Madison on I90: exit west at Highway 30. Turn right on Highway 113, Packers Avenue. At the first stoplight, turn right on International Lane and continue to the airport terminal.

Heading south to Madison on I90-I94: exit Highway 51 South, continue three miles. At the stoplight, turn right on Anderson Street. Follow Anderson until it ends, turn right on International Lane and continue to the airport terminal.

Heading south on Highway 51: three miles past Interstate 90-94, turn right on Anderson Street. Follow Anderson until it ends, turn right on International Lane and continue to the airport terminal.

Heading west from Milwaukee on I94: continue west to Madison on Highway 30. Turn right on Highway 113, Packers Avenue. At the first stoplight, turn right on International Lane and continue to the airport terminal.

(How to Get to the Airport, continued)

Heading northeast to Madison on Highway 18-151: turn right on Highway 12 at the beltline. Exit Highway 12 and follow Interstate 90 North, exiting at Highway 30. Turn right on Highway 113, Packers Avenue. At the first stoplight, turn right on International Lane and continue to the airport terminal.

Heading southwest to Madison on Highway 151: continue on Highway 151 South into Madison. The street name is East Washington Avenue Turn right on Stoughton Rd., which is also Highway 51 North. Turn left on Anderson Street, follow Anderson until it ends. Turn right on International Lane and continue to the airport terminal.

A cab ride to the airport costs $5–$15.

Greyhound
2 S Bedford Street
(608) 257-3050

Travel Agents
STA Travel
122 State Street
(608) 263-8810

Students Speak Out On...
Transportation

"Public transportation is great. If you are a student, you get a free bus pass every semester to ride the Madison buses."

Q "The bus system is always running, and **bus passes are free**."

Q "You **can get anywhere on the buses**. There's no mass transit rail system or anything—it is not needed. However, I always had a car, so I never used the buses."

Q "**It's very convenient**. The Madison Metro buses are great."

Q "You don't need to worry about public transportation because **everything you need is right on campus**."

Q "Public transportation is extremely easy to use in Madison. **There are about 50 bus routes that cover the entire city**."

Q "**Public bus passes are free for students,** and they travel everywhere. It's really nice, and a lot of students ride them!"

Q "There is a bus system that all students can use for free. **It's very convenient, if you can figure out the schedules**."

Q "It is pretty convenient, and as a student, **you get a bus pass that allows you to ride for free** during the school year."

Q "The bus system is available all night, and it is a very safe method of getting home. **It is great because it prevents a lot of drunk driving**."

Q "Public transportation is never convenient, and most of the time, **it pays just to walk**. However, in the extreme heat or cold, there is a free bus that runs up Bascom every few minutes. If someone really wanted to take the time, they could try to get to the west or east side taking the bus, but it would double travel time."

Q "**Transportation is awesome** unless you need to go somewhere that requires two transfer points."

Q "Madison has an excellent bus system. If you go here, **it's to your benefit to get to know it**. Make sure you pick up a free student bus card, too."

The College Prowler Take On...
Transportation

Students feel pretty content with the various transportation options at UW. The shuttle bus is probably one of the more popular options. Students are able to take this up the ominous Bascom Hill, and around to the farthest academic building on campus. The bus runs about every fifteen minutes beginning at 7 a.m., and goes till 11 p.m.

In general, most places on campus or off are within a walking distance. However, UW and the city of Madison offer ways for students to go farther distances in shorter amounts of time. Therefore, public transportation is very accessible. As a student, you get a free bus pass that is good through the semester. As long as you can read a bus schedule, you are good to go. Lots of people use the busses to get to campus, go to the mall, or catch a movie. There is also a free bus that circles the campus to take students to academic buildings that are a little farther away. Madison also has an abundance of cabs that are more than willing to drive you anywhere. Of course, they are more expensive than the buses, but when you have bags of groceries, it's worth it. Madison also offers ways to get out of the city or state. The airport is only a few miles from campus, as is the Greyhound bus station. Travel agents are also available to help students plan getaways. Bottom line is that wherever you may need to go, there will be some means of getting you there.

The College Prowler® Grade on

Transportation: B+

A high grade for Transportation indicates that campus buses, public buses, cabs, and rental cars are readily-available and affordable. Other determining factors include proximity to an airport and the necessity of transportation.

Weather

The Lowdown On...
Weather

Average Temperature:		Average Precipitation:	
Fall:	48°F	Fall:	2.6 in.
Winter:	16°F	Winter:	1.3 in.
Spring:	51°F	Spring:	3.9 in.
Summer:	70°F	Summer:	4.4 in.

Students Speak Out On...
Weather

"The weather is hot in the summer and very cold in the winter. Bring a heavy coat, gloves, and a hat for sure. Sometimes it snows a lot in the winter, but sometimes it doesn't. The cold is the worst part."

Q "**The lakes can whip up a stiff breeze in January** and February—I like it here because we have all four seasons in full force. I spent all summer here once, and I loved it. Sailing, swimming, biking, hiking, and walking around the lake is great."

Q "The weather this year wasn't so bad because the winter was mild, but it was pretty cold. But even if it is cold, it is **often sunny, so it doesn't get too depressing**."

Q "It is very cold in the winter, but it's not unbearable. I really do hate the cold, but **it's not so bad that it ruins the good times**. When it is nice, there is an amazing atmosphere, especially being on the two lakes. When it is warm, everyone hangs outside."

Q "The spring and summer are absolutely beautiful. **The winters are very harsh**, but this past year was not bad at all. It gets really cold in the winter, but there is nothing better than a beautiful spring day sitting at the Union terrace. That is a big hotspot when the weather is nice."

Q "**When it's hot, it's hot; and when it's cold, it's cold**. The transition times when the weather is nice rarely last more than a week or two."

Q "For the most part, we have all four seasons. It gets pretty cold in the winter, and because Madison is an isthmus that sits between two lakes, the lake wind is pretty bitter. Even though it does get cold in the winter, **it always has blue skies, which makes it okay**."

Q "**Weather can be great or it can suck**. The wind off the lake is harsh, but during the spring, it's worth it because the lake view is beautiful, especially from the terrace. It is gorgeous out there."

Q "The weather in Madison is typical Midwest weather—warm summers and cold winters. I am very impressed at how **clear they keep the sidewalks during the winter**. If we get a few inches of snow during the night, by the next morning the sidewalks are spotless."

Q "In the summer, the weather is either beautiful or humid. Fall is Madison's best season because its always crisp and just cool enough out. Winter can be harsh, so make sure you **have the warmest winter jacket** you can possibly find. Everyone in Madison either owns a Columbia or North Face winter jacket. Outside of that, wear what you want, and have clothing for a wide variety of weather."

The College Prowler Take On...
Weather

Weather is always going to be unpredictable, and weather in Madison is no exception. Students refer to UW's climate as mild fall and spring mixed with intense summer and winter. While this variation in temperatures can be annoying at times, students try to take it in stride. Students advise new students or visiting ones to come prepared for the temperamental weather.

Since Madison is located in the Midwest, the weather tends to change very quickly and dramatically. Summers can reach temperatures nearing 100 degrees, and winters can chill into the negative numbers. Walking to and from campus puts students outside, exposed for long amounts of time. In the winter gloves, hats, scarves, and boots are essential for trudging through snowy walkways. Summertime calls for less apparel but lots of sunscreen. Those attending UW should pack for every weather condition.

The College Prowler® Grade on
Weather: C

A high Weather grade designates that temperatures are mild and rarely reach extremes, that the campus tends to be sunny rather than rainy, and that weather is fairly consistent rather than unpredictable.

Report Card Summary

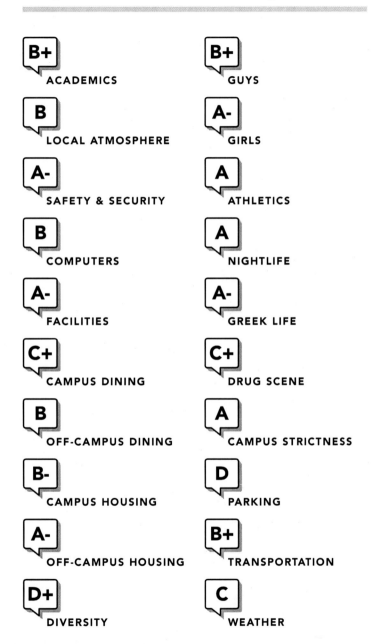

B+ ACADEMICS

B LOCAL ATMOSPHERE

A- SAFETY & SECURITY

B COMPUTERS

A- FACILITIES

C+ CAMPUS DINING

B OFF-CAMPUS DINING

B- CAMPUS HOUSING

A- OFF-CAMPUS HOUSING

D+ DIVERSITY

B+ GUYS

A- GIRLS

A ATHLETICS

A NIGHTLIFE

A- GREEK LIFE

C+ DRUG SCENE

A CAMPUS STRICTNESS

D PARKING

B+ TRANSPORTATION

C WEATHER

Overall Experience

Students Speak Out On...
Overall Experience

> "I have no regrets about coming here, and there is no place I would rather be at school. It is just so much fun that I don't even want to graduate. I am prolonging my time here! I love it too much!"

Q "I love Madison. **I have met great people from all over the country**. If I had to do it over, I wouldn't change a thing."

Q "It was good to go away, and I've met great people. I'm a theatre major, and I have met great people in that area so far. **Madison is a cool place to be**."

Q "I love Wisconsin. **It's an excellent university with a fun atmosphere**. I think I made the right choice in picking this university four years ago. If I had to go back and choose again, I would choose Wisconsin. I have had my highs and lows at this university, but that is to be expected with anything in life."

Q "Overall, **I couldn't be happier here**. I know of no one here who has transferred, and I never hear people complain. Classes here are incredibly hard, but once you find the balance between partying and studying you will never want to leave this school."

Q "Overall, I enjoy my days here. I never wish I was anywhere else. There's always something to do. College can be anything you want it to be. **Here, it's so big and there are so many choices**. The school definitely has a lot of nice people too."

Q "I love Madison and I am so happy I went there. There is **always something to do, and you are never bored**."

Q "I transferred here from the University of Pittsburgh, which was a very urban college—I wasn't really into it. I am so happy I chose UW-Madison; it is a great college that offers a lot of things for anybody. There are over 2,000 student organizations, so I'm sure there is something you can get into. **It's a great city and a very reputable school**, where a lot of great research and academic advancement comes from. Plus it is a great location—only three hours from Chicago and two from Milwaukee. I completely recommend UW. I think if anyone saw it, they would agree it is a good choice!"

Q "I love Madison and wouldn't want to be anywhere else. It was definitely one of the best decisions I made to go to Madison. **I have no regrets**."

Q "Overall, I loved Madison. I will probably live there once completing school. It's located on an isthmus between Lake Mendota and Lake Monona. There are trails that run along the lake to run and bike on. Madison is a very active campus athletically, intellectually, socially, and politically. On the whole, **I think this is the best campus in the nation**. If I were to go anywhere, only Stanford would come anywhere close to being considered."

Q "This is the best school. **I feel lucky that I came here**. I'm from NY and applied to all East Coast schools except for UW. I decided to come here without visiting the campus at all, and I couldn't have chosen a better school. The education is great. The people are great and the parties are unbelievable—especially at Chi Phi."

Q "Overall, the people are great in Wisconsin, and the motto here is pretty much **work hard, play hard**. The campus is a wet campus, so they serve beer at the student union, and there are tons of bars and parties within walking distance."

Q "I love it, but I've always wanted a large school. **I occasionally wish that it was more racially diverse**, but that argument can be made for most schools across the country."

Q "I had a rough time the first couple of semesters, but overall, **I know I couldn't be this happy anywhere else**. I love the amount of people that I meet daily, the weather when it is summer, and the view of the Isthmus at Sunset from Lake Mendota. With State Street as my front lawn, how could I not be glad to be here?"

Q "I have loved the school. I do not wish I were somewhere else, **although I miss home sometimes**."

Q "I could not dream of a better school than UW Madison.
**These are going to be the years of my life I look back
on and smile about**, and I have made some of my best
friends in the course of my life here."

Q "I did transfer to Madison in hopes of bettering my
'college experience' and I would say that Madison has
fulfilled that hope. I have been challenged academically,
met some amazing people, and gotten involved with a
few organizations. I honestly cannot think of another place
that I would want to be—except maybe the University
of Maui. **Madison encompasses opportunity and
expectations**. You are expected to do well, and that
success opens doors to amazing opportunities."

The College Prowler Take On...
Overall Experience

Students put a lot of time and energy into their undergraduate education. Luckily for those at UW, many feel it has been a positive experience. The college atmosphere, expansive campus, and intense academics are only some of the reasons students enjoy UW so much. Students feel they are able to form relationships with other students, as well as their professors. Furthermore, UW leaves them prepared for their future.

An individual's undergraduate experience is one of the most exciting times in their lives. It is often the first time they are away from parents and making serious decisions about their future. Therefore, it is essential to pick the best university to spend these busy years at. UW offers amazing academics, an inviting atmosphere, and energetic student body. Its location geographically makes is comfortable as well as gorgeous. The facilities are very accommodating, as is the transportation system. Though with any school, there are things that can be improved upon, and even changed. Diversity is a point of contention at UW, while smaller issues seem to arise when dealing with dorm food and parking. Even so, students generally leave the school feeling satisfied and prepared for what's to come. Wherever you deiced to spend your undergraduate years, definitely consider the University of Wisconsin as a practical and fulfilling option.

The Inside Scoop

The Lowdown On...
The Inside Scoop

UW Slang:

Know the slang, know the school. The following is a list of things you really need to know before coming to UW. The more of these words you know, the better off you'll be.

B'Dubs – BW3 restaurant.

Bascom – Bascom Hill.

Cap Foods – Capital Center Foods.

Cap Square – Capital Square.

Casa Bs – Casa Bianca restaurant, now known as Pizza Di Roma.

Chi-Town – Chicago.

College – College Library.

Frat Row – Langdon St.

Madtown – Madison.

State – State St.

Tyme Machine – ATM.

In general, names of streets, restaurants, buildings, and shops are cut to one word. Tutto Pasta is just Tutto and the Helen C. White Building is just Helen C.

Things I Wish I Knew Before Coming to UW

- The winters in the Midwest are as cold as people say, so come prepared.
- Bascom Hill is not really a hill but more of a huge upward incline. The walk up it sometime requires an intense amount of energy, especially at eight in the morning.
- There are tons of student organizations, so join one!
- The school provides you with a free bus pass for the city bus system.
- The Lakeshore path is an alternative to taking Bascom Hill.
- Athletic event tickets sell out fast.

Tips to Succeed at UW

Get involved. Students who take part in extra-curricular activities leave UW feeling more accomplished. These organizations are set up to help foster individual interests, and to help new students meet people. Do take advantage of them.

Don't be afraid to ask for help. Whether this falls into academics, personal issues, or career choices, UW offers many support systems. Advising counselors are always willing to discuss classes and other school-related issues. UHS also provides services for more personal problems, and of course physical health concerns.

UW is academically challenging, so try to stay focused. With all the other opportunities and experiences involved with a college, it is often hard to maintain your grades. If you find yourself faltering academically, try very hard to mend the problem, and fast. Once you are behind it can be quite difficult to catch up again.

School Spirit

School spirit is at a continuous high at UW. State Street alone offers at least five school paraphernalia stores. The University Bookstore also houses a large section of school wear, posters, keychains, and other necessary badger gear. Football games bring out the most amount of school spirit. Students attend these events decked out in red and white. Even if you're not at a sporting game, you will see students everywhere sporting their Badger-wear.

UW Urban Legends

During the 1960s, the UW campus was at its height for political protest. Somewhere along the line, a story spread that our maze-like Humanities Building was blown up. While there was a bomb scare at Science Hall, UW's academic buildings were never comprised due to explosives.

While the lakeshore path is one of the most beautiful places to take a stroll, students are weary of it after nightfall. Due to rumors of crimes and sexual assault, this area has earned the nighttime nickname of "rapeshore path."

Traditions

UW students love traditions. One of them is the annual Mifflin Street Block Party. Since 1960, residents on this street open their homes and liquor cabinets to anyone wanting to party. Bands are often hired for entertainment, and you can expect to find at least 10,000 student attendees.

The Halloween season is another time for UW tradition. The weekend after Halloween, students will swarm State Street dressed in their best costumes. It is literally a sight to see, as walking through the crowd is a near impossibility. It's okay, though, because wherever you are there is someone acting crazy or showing off his or her costumes.

While winter can be one of the worst times weather-wise, UW students try to make the most of it. Bascom Hill is perfect for sledding down, and students will use everything from notebooks to cardboard boxes to travel its slope.

The city of Madison also has some traditions to offer the students. During late spring, summer, and fall Capital Square is closed every Saturday for the Farmer's Market. Here students can buy fresh produce, handmade jewelry, wild flowers, and other craft items.

Finding a Job or Internship

The Lowdown On...
Finding a Job or Internship

UW offers several career advising programs throughout its specific schools. The earlier you get in touch with these offices, the easier it will be post-graduation. Even if you are a freshman coming in with no specific major, these people can connect you to different academic programs that may help spark an interest. For those already set on a career path, the counselors here will link you to information about your choice job, alumni already in the field, and internship opportunities.

Advice

For those unsure of what to major in, try cross-college advising. Their counselors are knowledgeable of several majors throughout the school and help you narrow down your search. If you do know what academic path you want to take, contact that school's career advising as soon as possible. These offices are set to provide students with other types of career information. They will have internship listings, a hiring employer database, and names of academic support groups.

Career Center Resources and Services

Business Career Center
3290 Grainger Hall
975 University Ave.
(608) 262-2550 (front desk)
(866) 436-3533 (toll-free employer hotline)
www.bus.wisc.edu/career

This office provides services for both undergraduate and graduate students. For undergraduates, they break the career search down into a year-by-year plan. Like the other advising offices, they offer counseling, internship listings, and connection to hiring employers.

College of Agricultural and Life Sciences Career Services
116 Agricultural Hall
1450 Linden Dr.
(608) 262-3003
asa@cals.wisc.edu
www.cals.wisc.edu/students/cswebmn

For those in the CALS, this office provides internship opportunities, career assessments, job-searching tips, and employer access.

Educational Placement and Career Services
B150 Education Building
1000 Bascom Mall
(608) 262-1755
Monday–Friday 7:45 a.m.–4:30 p.m.
www.careers.education.wisc.edu

Geared towards those looking to go into the education field, this center offer job fairs, career workshops, internship listings, and job search engines.

Engineering Career Services
www.ecs.engr.wisc.edu
ecs@engr.wisc.edu

This office is helpful for students going into engineering fields. They offer academic support, career counseling, internship information, and employment opportunities.

(Career Resources and Services, continued)

Letters & Science/Human Ecology Career Center

905 University Avenue, Suite 160

(608) 262-3921

www.lssaa.wisc.edu/careers

This is one of the largest academic resources at UW. They break down their services into those for students, alumni and employers. Of course these three groups overlap through the office's career counseling, internship listings, and employer connections.

Average Salary Information

Due the number and size of undergraduate schools at UW, there is no one office that keeps track of alumni salary. This information is voluntarily reported by exiting students. Here are the schools, however, who have kept track of alumni salary.

School of Business

$34,000–$60,000

College of Agricultural & Life Sciences

$14,000–$50,000

School of Law

$22,000–$200,000

School of Nursing

$43,000–$55,000

Alumni

The Lowdown On...
Alumni

Alumni Web Site:
www.uwalumni.com

Alumni Office:
Wisconsin Alumni Association
650 North Lake St.
Madison, WI 53706
(608) 262-2551
(888) WIS-ALUM
waa@uwalumni.com

Services Available:
WAA is essential for those leaving UW. This group provides an alumni directory, information on reunions, and dates for special alumni events. In terms of career aspects, WAA is part of a program that connects students with alumni already successful in their fields.

Major Alumni Events

Badger State Game Triathlon, UW Alumni Gold Special

Alumni Publications

Annual Report

This publication focuses on, "uniting alumni chapters, current students, affiliate groups, academic departments and the chancellor's office to better serve UW alumni and friends."

Resource Guide

For those who are members of the Wisconsin Alumni Association, this pamphlet discusses the various things like the benefits of being part of WAA, alumni travel trips, and alumni athletics teams.

Did You Know?

Famous UW Alumni:

George Poage (Class of 1903) – African American medal winner in track in the 1904 Olympics

Harry Steenbock (Class of '16) – Professor; discovered and patented Vitamin D

Jerry Bock (Class of '48) – Co-composer of *Fiddler on the Roof* and *Fiorello*

David W. Grainger (Class of '50) – Senior chairman, W W Grainger, Inc., Skokie, Ill.

Jim Lovell (Class of '50) – Astronaut, Apollo 13 mission

Jane Brody (Class of '63) – Health columnist, *New York Times*

Joan Cusack (Class of '84) – Actress (*Working Girl, In & Out, Grosse Pointe Blank*)

Famous Alumni Who Never Graduated:

Charles Lindbergh – Aviator who completed the first solo trans-Atlantic flight

Gena Rowlands – Actress

Frank Lloyd Wright – Architect

Student Organizations

UW offers an extensive number of student organizations. Students can find clubs geared towards anything from celebrating diversity to discussing new fiction. The following is a sample list of many of the organizations and clubs UW offers. See a full list of organizations at: *www.soo.studentorg.wisc.edu.*

Actuarial Science Club (UW)

Advertising Club (UW-Ad Club)

African Students Association (ASA)

AHANA Pre-Health Society

Aikikai-UW (Aikido club)

Allies Program (UW-Madison)

Alpha Chi Sigma (professional coed chemistry fraternity)

Alpha Pi Mu: Industrial Engineering Honor Society

American Institute of Aeronautics and Astronautics (AIAA)

American Institute of Chemical Engineers (AIChE)

American Library Association, UW Student Chapter (ALASC)

American Medical Student Association (AMSA)

Amnesty International

Anime Club

Arab Student Organization

Arts Administration Association

ASCE Concrete Canoe

Asian American Student Union (AASU)

Asian Christian Fellowship (ACF)

Aspiring Nurses Association

Association of Athletic Training Students (AATS)

Association of Information Systems Professionals (AISP)

Association of Women in Agriculture (AWA)

Badger Ballroom Dance Team (BBDT)

Badger Yearbook

Badminton Club

Ballroom Dance Association (UWBDA)

Biomedical Engineering Society (BMES)

Black Graduate and Professional Organization

Buddhists for World Peace

Budo Club

CALS Honors and Research Society (CHARS)

Campus Vegetarian Society

Capoeira Angola Madison

CARE Fellowship

Career Development Association (CDA)

Chabad Jewish Student Association

Chautauqua (Bradley Hall organization)

Chess Club (UW)

Chesterton Society

Children's Justice Project

China Economic Forum

Chinese Language and Culture Club

Chinese Undergraduate Student Assocation (CUSA)

Choi Tae Kwon Do Club

Christian Science Student Organization

Collegiate Forensics League of UW-Madison

Community Outreach and Advocacy for Refugees at the University of Wisconsin

Companion Animal Club (CAC)

Composers' Collective (UWCC)

CRY America, UW-Madison

Cultural Richness Empowers Women (CREW)

Curb Magazine

Cycling Club (UW)

DanceSport Team-UW (DST-UW)

Dialogue International

Dietetics and Nutrition Club

Disney College Program Alumni Association, UW-Madison

Eagle Claw Kung Fu Club (UW)

Economics Student Association (ESA)

Entrepreneurship Association

Environmental Field Trip Club

Ethics Club

Fencing Club (UWFC)

Figure Skating Club

Finance and Investment Society

Food Not Bombs Madison (FNB)

Habitat for Humanity (UW Chapter)

Health Education Leadership Program (HELP)

Health Professions Society (HPS)

Hillel at the University of Wisconsin-Madison

Hip-Hop's Last Hope (HHLH)

History Book Club

Holocaust Remembrance Coalition

Homecoming Committee (UW)

Homeless Cooperative

Hong Kong Students Association (HKSA)

Honors Student Organization (HSO)

HOPE

Human Development and Family Studies Graduate Student Organization

Human Factors and Ergonomics Society

IEEE Robot Team

Impact Movement

India Students Association

Indigenous Law Students Association (ILSA)

Indonesian Christian Fellowship (ICF)

Institute of Industrial Engineers (IIE)

Interior Designers' Club

Internal Medicine Interest Group

International Business Student Association (IBSA) / Rotaract Club

International Socialist Organization (ISO)

Italian Club

Jewish Cultural Collective (JCC)

Kendo Club (UW)

Korean American Students Association (KASA)

La Colectiva

Law School Family Association

Legal Studies Association (LSA)

Lifeskills

Lion's Club (UW-Madison)

Lutheran Campus Ministry at UW-Madison

Macintosh Users Group, UW-Madison (WiscMUG)

Mad City Skydivers (Skydiving Club, UW)

Madison Association of Turkish Students (MATS)

Madison Board Gamers

Malaysian Students Association (MSA)

Math Club

Medical Microbiology & Immunology Club (MMI Club)

Medical Students Association (MSA)

Mentorship Achievement Program (MAP)

Mexican Students Association (MEXSA)

Microbiology Club

Microfinance Society

Middle Eastern Law Students Association

Middleton House

Minority Affairs Program in Pharmacy (MAPP)

Mock Trial Team (UW-Madison)

Model United Nations

Moot Court Club

Multicultural Business Students Association (MBSA)

MultiCultural Student Coalition (MCSC)

Muslim Students' Association

National Lawyers Guild (UW Chapter)

National Society of Collegiate Scholars (NSCS)

Naval Reserve Officer Training Corps, UW-Madison

The Navigators at UW-Madison

Nelson Institute Forum

New Valaam Theological Academy

OB/Gyn Interest Group

Orthodox Christian Fellowship of Madison

Our Bodies, Our Rights!

PAVE (Promoting Awareness, Victim Empowerment)

Pediatric Interest Group

Polish Student Association

Polygon Engineering Student Council

Powerlifting Badgers (UW-Madison)

Pranic Healing Association (UW-Madison)

Pre-Dental Society (UW-PDS)

Pre-Law Society (PLS)

Pre-Occupational Therapy Student Organization

Public Interest Law Foundation (PILF)

Public Relations Student Society of America (PRSSA), UW-Madison

Quiz Bowl Team (UW)

Returned Peace Corps Volunteers of Madison Risk

Management and Insurance Society (RMIS)

Running Club (UW)

Rural Health Interest Group

Salvation Army Learning Center

Shorin Ryu Karate Club

Sierra Student Coalition

Sikh Student Association

Silver Wings, UW-Madison Branch

Sindisa AIDS Organization

Singapore Students Association (SSA)

SLICE: Students Living Inter-Cultural Experiences

Small Group Bible Studies-St. Paul's

Sober Students on Campus

Society for Human Resource Management (SHRM, UW-Madison)

Society of Professional Journalists, UW-Madison Chapter

Society of Women Engineers (SWE)

South Asia Forum (Madison)

Spanish Enthusiasts (UW-Madison)

Sportfishing Team (UW)

St. Paul's Alpha-Omega Undergrad Group

Student Action for Indian Volunteerism and Aid (SAIVA)

Student Alliance for Firearm Education and Responsibility

Student Chapter-Alliance of Veterinarians for the Environment (SAVE)

Student Faculty Board

Student Global AIDS Campaign (Madison Chapter SGAC)

Student Impact/Campus Crusade for Christ (UW Madison)

Students for a Free Tibet (SFT), UW

Students for Ashok Kumar

Students for Camp Heartland (SFCH)

Students for Equality

Students for New Urbanism (Madison)

Students for Social Welfare

Students for the Improvement of Urban Healthcare

Super Scrabble Society

Surgery Interest Group (SIG)

Tai Chi at UW-Madison

Taiwanese Student Association (TSA)

Tennis Club (UW-Madison)

Thai Student Association (TSA)

Theatre Arts

Tolkien and Fantasy Society

Transfer Student Organization, UW-Madison

Transportation Society (UWiTS)

Triathlon Team

TRUTH (Teaching Racial Understanding Through History)

UNICEF: UW-Madison

Vietnamese Student Association (VSA)

Wilderness Medical Society, UW-Madison

Wildlife Ecology Graduate Student Association

Wisconsin Alumni Student Board (WASB)

Wisconsin Black Student Union

Wisconsin Management Consulting Club

Wisconsin Medical Forum

Wisconsin Student Planning Association (WSPA)

Wisconsin Track Club

WISPIRG-WI Student Public Interest Research Group

Witte Student Organization

Women in Medicine (WIM)

WUD Distinguished Lecture Series (DLS)

WUD Film Committee

WUD Global Connections Committee

WUD Music Committee

Zen Dojo, UW

The Best & Worst

The Ten **BEST** Things About UW

1	Number of people
2	Expansive academic programs
3	Educational resources
4	Atmosphere
5	Number of student organizations
6	Number of career advising offices
7	Summertime
8	State Street
9	Student unions
10	Socialization opportunities

The Ten **WORST** Things About UW

1 Walking up Bascom hill during the winter

2 Distance to some academic buildings

3 Lack of diversity

4 Bar crowds

5 Lack of parking

6 The winters

7 Dorm room size

8 Dorm food

9 Lack of decent clubs

10 The wait time to get into some bars

Visiting

The Lowdown On...
Visiting

Hotel Information:

Best Western Inn
22 S Carroll St.
(608) 257-8811
Distance from Campus:
1.4 miles
Price Range: $89–$109

Best Western InnTowner
2424 University Ave.
(608) 233-8778
Distance from Campus:
1.6 miles
Price Range: $99–$200

Holiday Inn Express
722 John Nolen Dr.
(608) 255-7400
Distance from Campus:
3 miles
Price Range: $85–$140

University Inn
441 N Frances St.
(608) 285-8040
Distance from Campus:
0.9 miles
Price Range: $50–$150
(Closed during holidays)

Take a Campus Virtual Tour

www.news.wisc.edu/welcome/odyssey/Campus/tourstart

To Schedule a Group Information Session or Interview:

Campus Information and Visitor Center (CIVC)

1st Floor, Red Gym

716 Langdon Street

Madison, WI 53706

(608) 263-2400

askbucky@redgym.wisc.edu

Campus Tours

Walking tours are offered Monday–Friday beginning at 3 p.m., and Saturday–Sunday at noon. The tours last about 75 minutes and cover the majority of campus. Information sessions are also available for those interested in specific departments. Sessions last one hour and are presented for several departments. Be sure to call in advance to secure a spot for either event. This excludes University Holidays and home football game Saturdays.

Did You Know?

You can also take a **self-guided tour of campus**. Pick up tour materials at the Campus Information and Visitor Center inside the Red Gym at 716 Langdon Street.

Overnight Visits

Students and family are allowed to remain overnight while visiting Madison and the UW campus. The following are accommodations suggested by UW.

The Friedrick Center

1950 Willow Drive
(608) 231-1341
jffred@ecc.uwex.edu
Price: $62–$82

The Lowell Center

610 Langdon Street
(608) 256-2621
lowell@ecc.uwex.edu
Price: $67–$77

Short Course Office

116 Agriculture Hall
1450 Linden Drive
(608) 262-2270
dorms@cals.wisc.edu
Price: $14–$32 per person

Memorial Union (East campus)

800 Langdon Street
(608) 262-1583
Price: $55–$87

Union South (West campus)

227 N. Randall Ave.
(608) 263-2600
Price: $55–$87

Fluno Center for Executive Education

601 University Ave.
(877) 77-FLUNO
(608) 441-7220
reservations@fluno.com
Price: $135–$145

Directions to Campus

Driving from the North

- Start by going south on Interstate 39.
- Once near Madison, take exit number 1A; this will put you onto E. Washington Avenue, where you want to go right.
- Take this until N. Butler Street and turn right onto it.
- Butler Street brings your to Gorham Street. Turn left onto Gorham Street
- Stay on this road as it starts to turn into University Avenue and goes towards Park Street
- Once at Park Street, go right. This will bring you to Lathrop where you need to turn left.
- Lincoln Drive is a few blocks up on the right.

Driving from the South

- Start by taking Interstate 90 West.
- Interstate 90 becomes Interstate 39 North. You will have to pay highway tolls periodically.
- Once near Madison, merge onto exit number 142A; this will take put you on the West Beltine Highway.
- After a few miles merge onto John Nolen Drive, exit number 263; this will take you to North Shore Drive where you will turn left.
- Stay straight for a while, as this street turns into Regent Street
- Once on Regent go until you hit N. Park Street. Turn right onto.
- After Park Street, go to Lathrop Drive and take a left; then, turn right on Lincoln Drive

Driving from the East

- Start by going West on Interstate 94.
- Then take exit number 1A towards the Madison area.
- After this, merge onto WI-30 West.
- This will bring you to E. Washington Avenue. Take this street up towards the state capital.
- This goes towards N. Butler Street. Turn right onto it.
- Butler Street brings your to Gorham Street Turn left onto Gorham Street.
- Stay on this road as it starts to turn into University Avenue and goes towards Park Street.
- Once at Park Street, go right. This will bring you to Lathrop where you need to turn left, and Lincoln Drive is a few blocks up on the right.

Driving from the West

- Take Interstate 94 East until you get to right outside Madison, WI.
- Then, take the second exit, US-51 S via exit number 132, into Madison.
- After that, turn right onto US-151 S/E, which is also known as East Washington Avenue.
- From there, go straight until you reach N. Butler Street.
- On Butler take a right turn. This will take you to E. Gorham Street, where you will want to turn left.
- Gorham Street turns into University Avenue. Follow this until you hit Park Street. Turn right onto Park Street
- Park Street will take you to Lathrop Street where you will take a left. After this, Lincoln Drive is only a few blocks away..

Words to Know

Academic Probation – A suspension imposed on a student if he or she fails to keep up with the school's minimum academic requirements. Those unable to improve their grades after receiving this warning can face dismissal.

Beer Pong/Beirut – A drinking game involving cups of beer arranged in a pyramid shape on each side of a table. The goal is to get a ping pong ball into one of the opponent's cups by throwing the ball or hitting it with a paddle. If the ball lands in a cup, the opponent is required to drink the beer.

Bid – An invitation from a fraternity or sorority to 'pledge' (join) that specific house.

Blue-Light Phone – Brightly-colored phone posts with a blue light bulb on top. These phones exist for security purposes and are located at various outside locations around most campuses. In an emergency, a student can pick up one of these phones (free of charge) to connect with campus police or a security escort.

Campus Police – Police who are specifically assigned to a given institution. Campus police are typically not regular city officers; they are employed by the university in a full-time capacity.

Club Sports – A level of sports that falls somewhere between varsity and intramural. If a student is unable to commit to a varsity team but has a lot of passion for athletics, a club sport could be a better, less intense option. Even less demanding, intramural (IM) sports often involve no traveling and considerably less time.

Cocaine – An illegal drug. Also known as "coke" or "blow," cocaine often resembles a white crystalline or powdery substance. It is highly addictive and dangerous.

Common Application – An application with which students can apply to multiple schools.

Course Registration – The period of official class selection for the upcoming quarter or semester. Prior to registration, it is best to prepare several back-up courses in case a particular class becomes full. If a course is full, students can place themselves on the waitlist, although this still does not guarantee entry.

Division Athletics – Athletic classifications range from Division I to Division III. Division IA is the most competitive, while Division III is considered to be the least competitive.

Dorm – A dorm (or dormitory) is an on-campus housing facility. Dorms can provide a range of options from suite-style rooms to more communal options that include shared bathrooms. Most first-year students live in dorms. Some upperclassmen who wish to stay on campus also choose this option.

Early Action – An application option with which a student can apply to a school and receive an early acceptance response without a binding commitment. This system is becoming less and less available.

Early Decision – An application option that students should use only if they are certain they plan to attend the school in question. If a student applies using the early decision option and is admitted, he or she is required and bound to attend that university. Admission rates are usually higher among students who apply through early decision, as the student is clearly indicating that the school is his or her first choice.

Ecstasy – An illegal drug. Also known as "E" or "X," ecstasy looks like a pill and most resembles an aspirin. Considered a party drug, ecstasy is very dangerous and can be deadly.

Ethernet – An extremely fast Internet connection available in most university-owned residence halls. To use an Ethernet connection properly, a student will need a network card and cable for his or her computer.

Fake ID – A counterfeit identification card that contains false information. Most commonly, students get fake IDs with altered birthdates so that they appear to be older than 21 (and therefore of legal drinking age). Even though it is illegal, many college students have fake IDs in hopes of purchasing alcohol or getting into bars.

Frosh – Slang for "freshman" or "freshmen."

Hazing – Initiation rituals administered by some fraternities or sororities as part of the pledging process. Many universities have outlawed hazing due to its degrading, and sometimes dangerous, nature.

Intramurals (IMs) – A popular, and usually free, sport league in which students create teams and compete against one another. These sports vary in competitiveness and can include a range of activities—everything from billiards to water polo. IM sports are a great way to meet people with similar interests.

Keg – Officially called a half-barrel, a keg contains roughly 200 12-ounce servings of beer.

LSD – An illegal drug, also known as acid, this hallucinogenic drug most commonly resembles a tab of paper.

Marijuana – An illegal drug, also known as weed or pot; along with alcohol, marijuana is one of the most commonly-found drugs on campuses across the country.

Major –The focal point of a student's college studies; a specific topic that is studied for a degree. Examples of majors include physics, English, history, computer science, economics, business, and music. Many students decide on a specific major before arriving on campus, while others are simply "undecided" until declaring a major. Those who are extremely interested in two areas can also choose to double major.

Meal Block – The equivalent of one meal. Students on a meal plan usually receive a fixed number of meals per week. Each meal, or "block," can be redeemed at the school's dining facilities in place of cash. Often, a student's weekly allotment of meal blocks will be forfeited if not used.

Minor – An additional focal point in a student's education. Often serving as a complement or addition to a student's main area of focus, a minor has fewer requirements and prerequisites to fulfill than a major. Minors are not required for graduation from most schools; however some students who want to explore many different interests choose to pursue both a major and a minor.

Mushrooms – An illegal drug. Also known as "'shrooms," this drug resembles regular mushrooms but is extremely hallucinogenic.

Off-Campus Housing – Housing from a particular landlord or rental group that is not affiliated with the university. Depending on the college, off-campus housing can range from extremely popular to non-existent. Students who choose to live off campus are typically given more freedom, but they also have to deal with possible subletting scenarios, furniture, bills, and other issues. In addition to these factors, rental prices and distance often affect a student's decision to move off campus.

Office Hours – Time that teachers set aside for students who have questions about coursework. Office hours are a good forum for students to go over any problems and to show interest in the subject material.

Pledging – The early phase of joining a fraternity or sorority, pledging takes place after a student has gone through rush and received a bid. Pledging usually lasts between one and two semesters. Once the pledging period is complete and a particular student has done everything that is required to become a member, that student is considered a brother or sister. If a fraternity or a sorority would decide to "haze" a group of students, this initiation would take place during the pledging period.

Private Institution – A school that does not use tax revenue to subsidize education costs. Private schools typically cost more than public schools and are usually smaller.

Prof – Slang for "professor."

Public Institution – A school that uses tax revenue to subsidize education costs. Public schools are often a good value for in-state residents and tend to be larger than most private colleges.

Quarter System (or Trimester System) – A type of academic calendar system. In this setup, students take classes for three academic periods. The first quarter usually starts in late September or early October and concludes right before Christmas. The second quarter usually starts around early to mid–January and finishes up around March or April. The last academic quarter, or "third quarter," usually starts in late March or early April and finishes up in late May or Mid-June. The fourth quarter is summer. The major difference between the quarter system and semester system is that students take more, less comprehensive courses under the quarter calendar.

RA (Resident Assistant) – A student leader who is assigned to a particular floor in a dormitory in order to help to the other students who live there. An RA's duties include ensuring student safety and providing assistance wherever possible.

Recitation – An extension of a specific course; a review session. Some classes, particularly large lectures, are supplemented with mandatory recitation sessions that provide a relatively personal class setting.

Rolling Admissions – A form of admissions. Most commonly found at public institutions, schools with this type of policy continue to accept students throughout the year until their class sizes are met. For example, some schools begin accepting students as early as December and will continue to do so until April or May.

Room and Board – This figure is typically the combined cost of a university-owned room and a meal plan.

Room Draw/Housing Lottery – A common way to pick on-campus room assignments for the following year. If a student decides to remain in university-owned housing, he or she is assigned a unique number that, along with seniority, is used to determine his or her housing for the next year.

Rush – The period in which students can meet the brothers and sisters of a particular chapter and find out if a given fraternity or sorority is right for them. Rushing a fraternity or a sorority is not a requirement at any school. The goal of rush is to give students who are serious about pledging a feel for what to expect.

Semester System – The most common type of academic calendar system at college campuses. This setup typically includes two semesters in a given school year. The fall semester starts around the end of August or early September and concludes before winter vacation. The spring semester usually starts in mid-January and ends in late April or May.

Student Center/Rec Center/Student Union – A common area on campus that often contains study areas, recreation facilities, and eateries. This building is often a good place to meet up with fellow students; depending on the school, the student center can have a huge role or a non-existent role in campus life.

Student ID – A university-issued photo ID that serves as a student's key to school-related functions. Some schools require students to show these cards in order to get into dorms, libraries, cafeterias, and other facilities. In addition to storing meal plan information, in some cases, a student ID can actually work as a debit card and allow students to purchase things from bookstores or local shops.

Suite – A type of dorm room. Unlike dorms that feature communal bathrooms shared by the entire floor, suites offer bathrooms shared only among the suite. Suite-style dorm rooms can house anywhere from two to ten students.

TA (Teacher's Assistant) – An undergraduate or grad student who helps in some manner with a specific course. In some cases, a TA will teach a class, assist a professor, grade assignments, or conduct office hours.

Undergraduate – A student in the process of studying for his or her bachelor's degree.

ABOUT THE AUTHOR

Writing this book was one of the best experiences I've ever had. Being able to dedicate so much time and writing into a topic I care about is really rewarding. I am currently a senior at the University of Wisconsin, majoring in creative writing and philosophy. While both areas are challenging, I feel they really tie into and complement one another. The classes for both fields are amazing, as well. I am a native Minnesotan, so Madison isn't really that far from home for me. Even so, the distance has helped me to grow and mature. I truly hope this book offers you an insight to my school.

I would like to take a moment to thank a few people who helped me with this amazing project. Thank you Mommy, Papi, Jade, Bobby, Robert, Eric, Adam, the Blanchards, and everyone at College Prowler!

Nicole Rosario
nicolerosario@collegeprowler.com

California Colleges

California dreamin'?
This book is a must have for you!

CALIFORNIA COLLEGES
7¼" X 10", 762 Pages Paperback
$29.95 Retail
1-59658-501-3

Stanford, UC Berkeley, Caltech—California is home to some of America's greatest institutes of higher learning. *California Colleges* gives the lowdown on 24 of the best, side by side, in one prodigious volume.

New England Colleges

Looking for peace in the Northeast?
Pick up this regional guide to New England!

NEW ENGLAND COLLEGES
7¼" X 10", 1015 Pages Paperback
$29.95 Retail
1-59658-504-8

New England is the birthplace of many prestigious universities, and with so many to choose from, picking the right school can be a tough decision. With inside information on over 34 competive Northeastern schools, *New England Colleges* provides the same high-quality information prospective students expect from College Prowler in one all-inclusive, easy-to-use reference.

Schools of the South

Headin' down south? This book will help you find your way to the perfect school!

SCHOOLS OF THE SOUTH
7¼" X 10", 773 Pages Paperback
$29.95 Retail
1-59658-503-X

Southern pride is always strong. Whether it's across town or across state, many Southern students are devoted to their home sweet home. *Schools of the South* offers an honest student perspective on 36 universities available south of the Mason-Dixon.

Untangling
the Ivy League

The ultimate book for everything Ivy!

UNTANGLING THE IVY LEAGUE
7¼" X 10", 567 Pages Paperback
$24.95 Retail
1-59658-500-5

Ivy League students, alumni, admissions officers,
and other top insiders get together to tell it like it is.
Untangling the Ivy League covers every aspect—from
admissions and athletics to secret societies and urban
legends—of the nation's eight oldest, wealthiest, and
most competitive colleges and universities.

Tell Us What Life Is Really Like at Your School!

Have you ever wanted to let people know what your college is really like? Now's your chance to help millions of high school students choose the right college.

Let your voice be heard.

Check out *www.collegeprowler.com* for more info!

Need More Help?

Do you have more questions about this school?
Can't find a certain statistic? College Prowler is
here to help. We are the best source of college
information out there. We have a network
of thousands of students who can get the latest
information on any school to you ASAP.
E-mail us at info@collegeprowler.com with your
college-related questions.

E-Mail Us Your College-Related Questions!

Check out *www.collegeprowler.com* for more details.
1-800-290-2682

Write For Us!

Get published! Voice your opinion.

Writing a College Prowler guidebook is both fun and rewarding; our open-ended format allows your own creativity free reign. Our writers have been featured in national newspapers and have seen their names in bookstores across the country. Now is your chance to break into the publishing industry with one of the country's fastest-growing publishers!

Apply now at *www.collegeprowler.com*

Contact editor@collegeprowler.com or
call 1-800-290-2682 for more details.

Pros and Cons

Still can't figure out if this is the right school for you?
You've already read through this in-depth guide; why not
list the pros and cons? It will really help with narrowing down
your decision and determining whether or not
this school is right for you.

Pros	Cons
....	....
....	....
....	....
....	....
....	....
....	....
....	....
....	....
....	....
....	....
....	....
....	....
....	....

Pros and Cons

Still can't figure out if this is the right school for you?
You've already read through this in-depth guide; why not
list the pros and cons? It will really help with narrowing down
your decision and determining whether or not
this school is right for you.

Pros	Cons
....	....
....	....
....	....
....	....
....	....
....	....
....	....
....	....
....	....
....	....
....	....
....	....

Notes

....

....

....

....

....

....

....

....

....

....

....

....

....

Notes

....

....

....

....

....

....

....

....

....

....

....

....

....

Notes

··

··

··

··

··

··

··

··

··

··

··

··

··

Notes

....

....

....

....

....

....

....

....

....

....

....

....

....

Notes

....

....

....

....

....

....

....

....

....

....

....

....

....

Notes

···

···

···

···

···

···

···

···

···

···

···

···

···

Notes

....

....

....

....

....

....

....

....

....

....

....

....

....

Notes

....

....

....

....

....

....

....

....

....

....

....

....

....

Notes

....

....

....

....

....

....

....

....

....

....

....

....

....

Notes

....

....

....

....

....

....

....

....

....

....

....

....

....

Notes

....

....

....

....

....

....

....

....

....

....

....

....

....

Notes

....

....

....

....

....

....

....

....

....

....

....

....

....

Notes

....

....

....

....

....

....

....

....

....

....

....

....

....

Notes

....

....

....

....

....

....

....

....

....

....

....

....

....

Notes

·····································

·····································

·····································

·····································

·····································

·····································

·····································

·····································

·····································

·····································

·····································

·····································

·····································

Notes

....

....

....

....

....

....

....

....

....

....

....

....

....

Notes

....

....

....

....

....

....

....

....

....

....

....

....

....

Notes

....
....
....
....
....
....
....
....
....
....
....
....
....
....